Are you ready to have some fun?

Thank you so much for ordering the Pre-K YOUR Way Curriculum Series. I created these activities to support caring parents and teachers like you in creating meaningful learning experience for your children. I hope you enjoy these activities as much as I enjoyed creating them.

Please contact me with any questions or comments that you have while working through the curriculum booklet. I want to hear from **YOU!**

If you enjoy these activities, please write a review on the product that you purchased. All products can be found at:

www.jdeducational.com

Happy Playing, Learning and Growing!

Sincerely,

Jeana Kinne

Copyright@2018 Jeana Kinne/JDEducational

Pre-K YOUR Way Curriculum Series Materials may not be copied or distributed without written permission of JDEducational. Additional curriculum can be purchased at www.jdeducational.com

All rights reserved

ISBN-13: 978-1723580185

DEDICATION

This Curriculum Series is dedicated to all parents and teachers striving to provide optimal learning opportunities for the children in their care. Thank you for your patience, love and support in nurturing little minds, creating a positive impact on our future generations.

DISCLAIMER

JDEducational and the author is not to be held responsible for injury or damage created or caused while preparing for or completing the activities in this book. Adult supervision, safety and caution should be used at all times. Do not leave children unattended while completing these activities.

Pre-K Your Way Activity Series

© 2018 JDEducational
Curriculum Series materials may not be copied or distributed without written permission of JD Educational. Additional curriculum can be purchased at www.jdeducational.com

About Our Curriculum

Our Curriculum is designed to strengthen school readiness by meeting the identified skills and concepts, which are necessary for a smooth transition to Kindergarten. These curriculum modules include low-cost/no-cost activities which parents, preschool staff and home daycare providers can use with the children in their care.

This curriculum was developed using current Kindergarten Readiness Assessments including: Common Core Kindergarten Standards, the Preschool Learning Foundation and the Desired Results Developmental Profile.

This curriculum addresses the following areas of development:

- Cognitive Development
- Mathematical Development
- Physical Development
- Language Development
- Literacy Development
- Social-Emotional Development
- Self-Help Skill Development

This curriculum was developed to meet the interests of all children and based on the multiple intelligences theory by Howard Gardner. Gardner was a Harvard University Professor who believed that traditional education wasn't utilizing the strengths of all children. Every child is unique and learns differently. Gardner identified eight different "intelligences" and pathways to learning.

These eight intelligences include:

1. Linguistic – "word smart"
2. Logical-Mathematical – "numbers/reasoning smart"
3. Spatial - "picture smart"
4. Bodily-Kinesthetic – "movement smart"
5. Musical – "Rhythms and songs smart"
6. Interpersonal – "People smart"
7. Intrapersonal – "Self smart"
8. Naturalist – "outdoors/nature smart"

Learning Objectives - Level 1

These activities have been developed to meet specific, age-appropriate, Kindergarten-Readiness skills. These skills are laid out in the learning objectives of each activity. The following activities may be completed in any order desired and are specifically designed to address the academic domains: math, science, language, literacy, cognitive, problem solving, and social-emotional development. **After completing all modules in the Level 1 Curriculum Series, the child should be able to:**

Mathematics

- Name and recognize familiar shapes.
- Finish simple patterns using two elements.
- Count up to 5 objects.
- Recognize the names of numerals.

Problem Solving/Science and Investigation

- Identify three or more colors.
- Sort objects by one quality (characteristic i.e. Size, color)
- Name body parts and their function.
- Understand Different vs. Same.
- Classify objects by at least two properties.

Language

- Participate in familiar routines.
- Understand rules and expectations related to specific places and environments.
- Use words and gestures to communicate with same aged peers.
- Demonstrate awareness of the meaning of the behaviors of others.
- Use words to problem solve and respond to a variety of social situations.

Social/Emotional Development

- Understand and follow familiar safety routines.
- Demonstrate awareness of personal care routines.
- Develop and use self-regulation techniques.
- Acknowledge own feelings and respond with appropriate behaviors.
- Identify feelings in others.
- Engage with peers in an appropriate way (Depending on age and skill level).

JDEducational
Play · Learn · Grow

Table of Contents
Each unit builds on concepts learned in the previous unit.
Activities within each unity may be completed in any order desired.

Introduction .... Pg. 1 - 12

Unit 1: All About Me and Going on a Walk…. Pg. 13

- All About Me Themed Items For Indoor Learning Environment
- All About Me Kindergarten Readiness Themed Activities
- A1. Humans and Basic Needs
- A2. My Favorites _____
- A3. Hello Me
- A4. Spoon Walk
- A5. Hair on my Head
- A6. How Many Body Parts?
- A7. Eyeball Color Match
- A8. Body Beats
- A9. Pattern See
- A10. Name Game
- **Parenting Tips: Helping Children Understand Diversity…pg. 36**

Unit 2: My Family and My Environment …. Pg. 46

- A1. My Family Age
- A2. Family Photo
- A3. Family Tree
- A4. Different vs. Same Name
- A5. Last Name Letters
- A6. My Family Is
- A7. Family Match
- A8. Family Homes
- A9. Bucket Name
- A10. Family Pick Up
- **Parenting Tips: Taking Turns with Loved Ones…pg. 70**

Unit 3: Learning with Books….Pg. 80

- A1. Letter Search
- A2. Picture Hunt
- A3. Color Browse
- A4. Alphabetical
- A5. Classification
- A6. How Many
- A7. Books of Feelings
- A8. Name Full of Letters
- A9. My Age in Numbers
- A10. Spelling My Family
- **Parenting Tips: Teaching Indoor vs. Outdoor Expectations…pg. 102**

© JDEducational: Pre-K Your Way: Level 1 Book

Unit 4: Discovering My Five Senses....Pg. 112

- A1. Texture Sort
- A2. Tasting Colors
- A3. Hearing Voices
- A4. Smelling My World
- A5. Seeing Opposites
- A6. Matching Sounds
- A7. Color My Voice
- A8. Music Maker
- A9. Toe, Touch, Feel
- A10. See My Way
- **Parenting Tips: Supporting Age Appropriate Behavior...pg. 134**

Unit 5: Learning at the Park....Pg. 143

- A1. Blast Off
- A2. Stair Numbers
- A3. Word Kick
- A4. Hula Move
- A5. I Dig
- A6. Swing Me
- A7. Park Art
- A8. New Friend Meet
- A9. Number Chase
- A10. Ready, Listen
- **Parenting Tips: Creating Successful Transitions...pg. 165**

Unit 6: Investigating Nutrition....Pg. 174

- A1. Food Groups
- A2. Ready, Eat!
- A3. Colors of My Fruit
- A4. My Favorite Meal
- A5. Food that Grows
- A6. The Itty Bitty Seed
- A7. Egg, Scramble, Roll
- A8. Food Mix
- A9. Menu Mix
- A10. Recipe Delight
- **Parenting Tips: Trying New Foods...pg. 196**

More JDEducational Products .... Pg. 197

About the Author .... Pg. 208

Setting up an Indoor Learning Environment at Home

Home-based learning environments tend to be one of the most complicated and multi-functional spaces in a home. Not only do parents need to make room for the variety of crafts, toys and other materials, there also needs to be space for adults. A home is not only for learning and growing, but also a place where spending time together as a family is key. So, as a parent, where do you put all of this stuff without it taking over the entire home? Creating a simple, organized and mess-free play space is a large task, but with some pre-planning, it is possible.

Finding that "right" space where there isn't a lot of foot traffic is extremely important. Spend two days observing the common areas of your home. While doing this, make some mental notes as to what areas aren't used often and where adults tend to gather. If there's a corner or a wall of a common room that isn't needed on a regular basis, that's the perfect spot for a play area. When a child is playing, she/he is tapping into their creativity and telling a story. Waiting until the child finishes their play allows that child to complete their story they were creating, whether it's with a baby doll, building blocks, cars and trains - or another favorite toy. Completing tasks without constant interruptions will allow a child to form a beginning, middle and end (a full-circle) of play.

Next, what you should place in this learning environment is dependent on the child's age and developmental level. A toddler will play with something different then a five year old. No matter what age the child is, there are certain "must haves" for their space. These include: a quiet spot (either a bean bag or large pillow), books, puzzles, stuffed animals or baby dolls, an assortment of blocks, art materials and plastic or wood animals. When there are multiple-aged children in your home, be sure to give each one their own space, either by separating their areas - or using two different types of shelving units to visually demonstrate what is their

Organizing materials into functional and workable environments will support the process of learning in a practical, step-by-step fashion. This ensures that the space is easily kept clean and visually pleasing. Each toy should have it's own dedicated space. For small objects, sort them by category and place them in small baskets or plastic bins (balls, cars and trucks, train tracks, books, paper, crayons, etc). If possible, take a picture of the items when they're separated and attach the pictures to their appropriate bin or basket. These containers can be placed on the floor or in a shelving unit against the wall. Provide a children's table, or allow them to take artwork to the main table in your home.

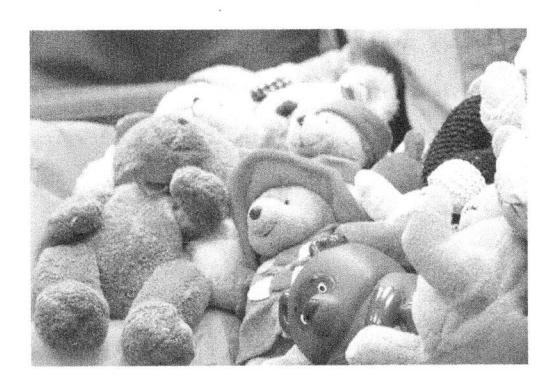

Sometimes children have too many different toys, which can cause toy chaos. Pick out no more than ten to twelve toys, which fall into the categories listed in the above paragraph. Place the rest of the items into large plastic storage bins and put them in a closet, garage or outdoor shed. Children will get bored when they play with the same toys over and over again. A typical toy rotation schedule is every three to four weeks, although some children get tired of toys quicker than others. If you notice the child becomes less engaged with the materials that are set out, rotate them with some of the materials that you put into storage bins. Watch as the child rediscovers their love for a toy they had previously lost interest in.

Lastly, learning to put away toys and stay organized at an early age helps prevent clutter over time - and will also teach children respect for their items. To make sure that the child takes ownership and pride in keeping the play area clean from the start, insist that they every time they are finished with a project or an activity in their play area, they clean up before they transition to another part of the home. Remember to always praise them with "Thank you for listening" or "Wow, you did that all by yourself" when they finish.

If clean up time is a struggle, encourage them to clean up by trying these ideas:

- **Play a clean-up game:** Using your watch, have a race against the clock! How long will it take them to put the toys away?

- **Sing a Song:** The Barney "Clean- Up" Song is a very popular choice.

- **Use this time as a Teachable Moment:** "Let's put all of the red things away first! Can you find all the red items?"

- **Help Out:** Having some help from a parent tends to be a motivator. "You put the trucks away and I will put the balls away".

Themed Learning Areas

Books: Age-appropriate books that directly correlate with the monthly theme can be found at your local library or bought separately online. This is a great opportunity to take a trip with your child to your local library and go on a search together. Have them identify words or pictures on the cover of children's books that correlate to the theme. Place a variety of books related to the theme in your child's book area. This will increase opportunities for them to expand their knowledge and use what they learn in the activities to comprehend what they read in the books.

Art Area: Encourage your child use this throughout each day by rotating items in an art area. These can be items have already been painted on, paper that they drew on already or leftover materials from another project. Thought provoking art projects are created when children are given unlimited opportunities to explore a variety of materials.

Some suggestions for the art area include:
- Crayons
- Paper
- Pens
- Empty Boxes (all kinds)
- Empty Toilet Paper or Paper Towel Rolls
- Foil
- Clean Q-tips for painting
- Scraps of paper
- Scraps of Yarn
- Scraps of any type of material – including fabric, sand paper, etc.
- Paper Bags
- Straws
- Popsicle Sticks
- Anything else that can be reused

Dramatic Play Area

This play area allows children to understand and experience the adult world through imitation and creativity. The dramatic play area provides a safe space for young children to create stories while practicing new vocabulary and practicing social skills. It is also a space where groups of children engage in pretend play which provides opportunities to learn self-help skills, share space and materials, take turns and the use abstract thinking. Each month there is a list of suggested materials to integrate into this area, which correlate with the theme of the month.

Suggested props to include in the dramatic play/pretend play area include:

- Clothes for Different Seasons
- Photos of Family Members
- Photos of Pets
- Pretend Food/Kitchen Items
- Books about different People
- Photo Albums
- The Child's Name written on different items
- Favorite Items that the child has.
- Dress-up clothes.
- Pretend Camera
- Blank Cards

JDEducational
Play · Learn · Grow

Pre-K YOUR Way
Level 1 Unit 1

All About Me; Understanding Diversity

Unit 1: All About Me Themed Academic Activities

These activities have been developed to meet specific, age-appropriate, Kindergarten-Readiness skills. These skills are specified in the learning objectives of each activity. The following activities may be completed in any order desired and are specifically designed to address the academic domains: math, science, language, literacy, cognitive, problem solving, and social-emotional development.

Each activity is on its own page. If the adult chooses to print the activities, the space below each activity is provided for adults to write notes regarding the activity. Adults are encouraged to note if the child enjoyed the activity and if the child needs to work on specific learning objectives. Each activity can be repeated more than once to enable the child to master the learning objectives designed for that activity.

All About Me Activities

1. Humans and Basic Needs
2. My Favorite _____.
3. Hello Me! Photo Order
4. Spoon Walk
5. Oh the Hair on my Head
6. How Many of Me
7. Eyeball Colors
8. Body Beats
9. Pattern See
10. Name Game

A1. Humans and Basic Needs - Activity time: 20 minutes

Materials Needed
- ☐ One (1) Pillow
- ☐ One (1) Cup the child can drink from
- ☐ One (1) Favorite Snack
- ☐ One (1) Blanket
- ☐ One (1) Empty Box

Instructions:

Step 1: Tell the child they're part of the **human race**.

Step 2: Have the child repeat after you, filling in the **number** of each body part:

" I'm a human and my name is __(fill in their name)__.

I have __(how many)__ eyes,

__(how many)__ ears and

__(how many)__ mouth.

I have __(how many)__ hands

and __(how many)__ feet.

I love and laugh and eat and play, and there is a lot more to me."

Step 3: Tell the child that all humans need **five things** to survive. They are:

1) Food
2) Water
3) Sleep
4) Warmth
5) Shelter

Step 4: The adult should place all materials (listed in the materials list) on the floor (pillow, cup, snack, blanket and empty box).

Step 5: Ask the child if they can tell you what each item is for. Example:

1) Food - Eat
2) Water - Drink
3) Pillow - Sleep
4) Blanket - Warmth
5) Shelter – Dry

Step 6: Ask the child why they need those things.

Example:

1) Food – Eat – So I'm not Hungry ("I have food to eat so I'm not hungry").
2) Water – Drink – So I'm not Thirsty
3) Pillow – Sleep – So I'm not Tired
4) Blanket – Warmth – So I'm not Cold
5) Shelter – Dry – So I'm not Wet

Step 7: Next tell the child you're going to play a listening game! Count each finger on one hand: 1,2,3,4,5. They have **five** fingers!

Step 8: Ask them to count the objects on the floor: 1,2,3,4,5. There are **five** objects!

Step 9: Tell the child to pick up the object that goes with what you say:

Example: Adult says "I am so hungry. I want to Eat _____". Child responds by picking up the Food.

<u>Adult says:</u>	<u>Child picks up:</u>
I want to Eat _____.	Food
I need to Sleep with my_____.	Pillow
I really need a _____ to Drink	Cup
Brrr… I am freezing! I need a _____ to keep me warm	Blanket
It is raining outside! I need to hide in a _____ to have Shelter	Empty Box

© JDEducational: Pre-K Your Way: Level 1 Book

A.1 Learning Objectives

Math/Science
- Count up to 5 objects.

Language/Literacy
- Use words and gestures to communicate.
- Use Language in Conversations.
- Demonstrate awareness of the meaning of the behaviors of others.
- Use words to problem solve and respond to a variety of social situations.

Problem Solving
- Sort objects by name and purpose.
- Classify objects.

Notes: What did your child do well? Are there any skills they need to continue to work on?

A2. My Favorite _____ - Activity time: 20 minutes

Materials Needed
☐ One (1) Box of Crayons ☐ One (1) Pen ☐ Three (3) Blank Pieces of Paper

Instructions:

Step 1: Tell the child that you're going to create a book together.

Step 2: The adult should write one of the following words at the top of each piece of blank paper:

1. Food
2. Toy
3. Place

Step 3: Have the child use the crayons to draw a picture of their favorite (food, toy, place) on the corresponding piece of paper.

Step 4: The adult should ask the child what they drew.

Step 5: The adult should use a pen to write down what the child says on each piece of paper.

Step 6: Ask the child to "Read" the book to you. Have them repeat:

"My Favorites" By (child's name)

My favorite food is_____.

My favorite toy is _____.

© JDEducational: Pre-K Your Way: Level 1 Book

My favorite place is _____.

Step 7: Re-read the "story" throughout the week.

Optional: Are there any other "favorites" that the child wants to add to the book? Have them draw a picture and tell the adult what it is.

A.2 Learning Objectives

Math/Science	Language/Literacy	Fine Motor
• N/A	• Use words and gestures to communicate. • Introduction to how pictures are used for a story.	• Using crayons to draw photos/representations

Notes: What did your child do well? Are there any skills they need to continue to work on?

A3. Hello Me - Activity time: 15 minutes

Materials Needed
- ☐ One (1) Box of Crayons
- ☐ One (1) Blank Piece of Paper
- ☐ One (1) printed picture of the child for each of the following ages:
  - ○ Newborn
  - ○ Six months
  - ○ One year
  - ○ Eighteen months
  - ○ Two years
  - ○ Present picture

Instructions:

Step 1: Place all the pictures on a table.

Step 2: Ask the child if they can identify who the child is in the pictures.

Step 3: Tell the child that all of those pictures are of them when they were little and there is one from today.

Step 4: Ask the child if to the pictures in order from youngest (baby photo) to oldest child (photo of them now).

Step 5: Ask the child if they can put the pictures in order from oldest child (picture of them now) to youngest photo (baby photo).

Step 6: Ask the child to count how many photos there are (Answer: total = 6).

Step 7: Ask the child to tell you one thing they like about each photo.

Step 8: Ask the child to draw a photo of themselves using crayons.

Step 9: Ask your child to tell you about their photo. Ask identifying questions such as:

- What color eyes do you have?
- What color is your hair?
- Where are your hands?
- What are you wearing in your photo?

© JDEducational: Pre-K Your Way: Level 1 Book

A.3 Learning Objectives

Math/Science
- Name and recognize people.
- Count up to 5 objects.

Language/Literacy
- Use words and gestures to communicate.
- Demonstrate awareness similiarities and differences.

Problem Solving
- Sort objects by one quality (characteristic).

Notes: What did your child do well? Are there any skills they need to continue to work on?

A4. Spoon Walk - Activity time: 20 minutes

Materials Needed
- ☐ Two (2) Empty paper or plastic cup
- ☐ One (1) Plastic spoon
- ☐ Eight (8) Cheerios (or other small cereal)

Instructions:

Step 1: Tell the child they're going to practice balance and coordination skills.

Step 2: The adult should place eight Cheerios in one plastic cup.

Step 3: Place the plastic cup, at the child's level, on one side of a room.

Step 4: The adult should place the empty plastic cup on the other side of the empty room.

Step 5: Tell the child to hold the spoon in one hand and place a Cheerio onto the plastic spoon.

Step 6: Tell the child to spin around in a circle three times, keeping the Cheerio on the spoon. Help the child count to three.

Step 7: Tell the child to walk across the room to the empty plastic cup, keeping the Cheerio on the spoon.

Step 8: Once the child reaches the other cup, tell them to tip the spoon into the cup so the Cheerio falls in the cup.

Step 9: Repeat steps 5 through 8 until the child has moved all of the Cheerios.

Optional: Repeat as many times as you want. Have the child count the steps it takes to get from one cup to the other.

A.4 Learning Objectives

Math/Science
- Count using one to one correspondence.
- Count up to 5 or more.

Language/Literacy
- Understand rules and expectations.
- Use words and gestures to communicate.

Gross/Fine Motor
- Gross Motor: Balance and Corrdination
- Fine Motor: Motor Planning

Notes: What did your child do well? Are there any skills they need to continue to work on?

A5. Hair on my Head - Activity time: 20 minutes

Materials Needed
- ☐ One (1) mirror (wall mounted or hand held)
- ☐ One (1) box of crayons
- ☐ One (1) Piece of blank paper

Instructions:

Step 1: Tell the child to look in the mirror and tell the adult what they see.

Step 2: Ask the child:

- What color eyes do you have?
- How many mouths do you have?
- How many noses do you have?
- How many ears do you have?
- What is the color hair do you have?
- Is your hair long or short?

Step 3: Have the child sit down at a table. Place the crayons and paper in front of them.

Step 4: Tell the child to draw a picture of themselves, just like how they look in the mirror.

Step 5: When the child is finished, ask the child:

- What color eyes do you have?
- Do you have hair?
- What color is your hair?
- Is your hair long or short?
- How many mouths do you have?
- How many noses do you have?
- How many ears do you have?

Step 6: Have the child hold up the picture they drew, and then look in the mirror. Does the child in the mirror look the similar to the child in the picture?

Step 7: Write your child's name on their photo using a crayon.

© JDEducational: Pre-K Your Way: Level 1 Book

Step 8: Ask your child to trace their name with a different color crayon.

A.5 Learning Objectives

Math/Science	Language/Literacy	Problem Solving
• Count up to 5 objects. • Counting by Category	• Use words and gestures to communicate. • Recognize their own name.	• Identify three or more colors. • Name body parts and their function.

Notes: What did your child do well? Are there any skills they need to continue to work on?

A6. How Many Body Parts? - Activity time: 20 minutes

> **Materials Needed**
> ☐ Two (2) Pieces of sidewalk chalk
> ☐ One large, safe outdoor space where you can draw with sidewalk chalk

Instructions:

Step 1: Have the child lay on their back, on the sidewalk.

Step 2: The adult should use sidewalk chalk to trace the child's body. Make sure to trace each of your child's fingers so they will be able to see **all ten fingers.**

Step 3: Ask the child stand up and use a piece of sidewalk chalk to draw their clothes and facial features on the outline of themselves.

Step 4: Ask the child to count how many of the following body parts they have:

1. Feet
2. Ears
3. Fingers
4. Toes
5. Knees
6. Arms
7. Elbows
8. Neck

Step 5: The adult should write the child's name next to the outline.

Step 6: Encourage the child to trace his/her name with another piece of sidewalk chalk.

© JDEducational: Pre-K Your Way: Level 1 Book

A.6 Learning Objectives

Math/Science	Language/Literacy	Problem Solving
• Count up to 5 objects.	• Understand that letters make words. • Spell your own name. • Trace letters	• Name body parts and their function. • Deomonstrate knowledge of yourself.

Notes: What did your child do well? Are there any skills they need to continue to work on?

A7. Eyeball Color Match - Activity time: 15 minutes

Materials Needed
- ☐ One (1) Box of crayons
- ☐ Two (2) 3x5 index cards

Instructions:

Step 1: Tell the child that everyone has **2 eyes**. The two index cards are going to represent two eyes.

Step 2: Ask the child to draw a picture of one eye on each index card.

Step 3: Tell the child to look at everyone's eyes in their family. Use the color crayon that matches the family member's eyes to draw one tally mark on each 3x5 index card.

For example: if mom has blue eyes, have the child draw one tally mark on both 3x5 index card with the blue crayon.

Step 4: Repeat Step 3 for every person in the home.

Step 5: Tell the child that although **all of the eyes are different colors**, they work in the same way. They help people **see**.

Step 6: Ask the child to count how many tally marks for each color there are.

A.7 Learning Objectives

Math/Science	Language/Literacy	Problem Solving
• Count up to 5 objects. • Recognize the names of numerals.	• Use words and gestures to communicate.	• Identify three or more colors. • Sort objects by one quality (characteristic i.e. Size, color) • Name body parts and their function. • Understand Different vs. Same. • Classify objects by at least two properties.

Notes: What did your child do well? Are there any skills they need to continue to work on?

A8. Body Beats - Activity time: 25 minutes

Materials Needed
☐ Two (2) Popsicle sticks

Instructions:

Step 1: Tell the child to stand up and hold one popsicle stick in each hand.

Step 2: Tell them they're going to use the popsicle sticks to **tap** a part of their body that the adult **names**. They need to use their listening ears to hear what the adult says.

Step 3: The adult should say, "Tap your ___(say one of the following)___":

- Ears
- Nose
- Feet
- Shoulders
- Knees
- Elbows
- Wrists
- Hair

Step 4: Are there other parts of the body that the child can name?

Step 5: The adult should name different body parts in the order of a **two-part pattern**, requesting children to tap them when named. See following for suggestions:

1. Ears, Nose, Ears, Nose, Ears, Nose
2. Feet, Shoulders, Feet, Shoulders, Feet, Shoulders
3. Knees, Elbows, Knees Elbows, Knees, Elbows
4. Wrists, Hair, Wrists, Hair, Wrists, Hair

Step 6: Can the child remember three-part patterns? See if they can remember the following sequences to "tap":

1. Ears, Nose, Feet, Ears, Nose, Feet, Ears, Nose, Feet
2. Shoulders, Knees, Elbows, Shoulders, Knees, Elbows, Shoulders, Knees, Elbows
3. Wrists, Hair, Ears, Wrists, Hair, Ears, Wrists, Hair, Ear

A.8 Learning Objectives

Math/Science
- Finish simple patterns using two elements.

Language/Literacy
- Follow simple directions.

Problem Solving
- Name body parts and their function.

Notes: What did your child do well? Are there any skills they need to continue to work on?

A9. Pattern See - Activity time: 15 minutes

Materials Needed
- ☐ Three (3) Pieces of Blank Piece of Paper
- ☐ One (1) Box of Crayons
- ☐ One (!) Pair of Adult sized scissors

Instructions:

Step 1: Tell the child that together, you're going to make a pattern.

Step 2: Tell the child to look at all of the clothes they are wearing. Ask the child to pick **three colors** that are on their clothes.

Step 3: Tell them to color the pieces of paper (one color for each piece of paper) with the color crayons that are the same color of clothing items they chose from Step 2.

Step 4: The adult should use adult scissors to cut each piece of paper in half.

Step 5: Have the child make a 3-part pattern with the colored paper.

For example:

- **Blue,** green, **blue,** , green

Step 6: Repeat Steps 1 though 6 with colors that other people in the home are wearing.

© JDEducational: Pre-K Your Way: Level 1 Book

A.9 Learning Objectives

Math/Science	Language/Literacy	Problem Solving
• Finish simple patterns using two elements. • Count up to 5 objects.	• Use words and gestures to communicate. • Follow New Directions.	• Identify three or more colors. • Sort objects by one quality (characteristic i.e. Size, color)

Notes: What did your child do well? Are there any skills they need to continue to work on?

A10. Name Game - Activity time: 15 minutes

Materials Needed
- ☐ One (1) Box of Markers
- ☐ One (1) Pen
- ☐ One (1) Piece of Paper

Instructions:

Step 1: The adult should use a pen to write the child's first name on a piece of paper.

Step 2: Ask the child what their favorite color is.

Step 3: Have the child find that color marker.

Step 4: Tell the child to decorate their name with their favorite color by drawing circles, triangles or squares around each letter in their name.

See picture below:

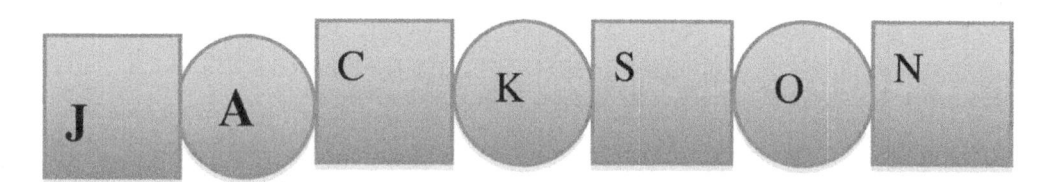

Step 5: Can they make a pattern with the shapes to decorate their names?

A.10 Learning Objectives

Math/Science	Language/Literacy	Problem Solving
• Name and recognize familiar shapes. • Finish simple patterns using two elements. • Count up to 5 objects.	• Use words and gestures to communicate with same aged peers. • Spell their name • Letter Identification	• N/A

Notes: What did your child do well? Are there any skills they need to continue to work on?

Behavior Tips - Understanding Diversity

Objective:

The purpose of Parenting Tips is to provide ideas and strategies that guide you in supporting your children to reach age appropriate social and emotional milestones. Social and Emotional Milestones include the following:

> **Social/Emotional Development**
> - Understanding safety routines.
> - Understanding personal care routines.
> - Develop self-regulation techniques.
> - Acknowledge feelings and appropriate behaviors.
> - Understand and identify feelings.
> - Understands age appropriate social interactions.
> - Communicates through words.

Introduction:

Understanding diversity is a complicated subject, especially when working with young children. Young children tend not to notice differences in race or ethnicity. Instead, at this young age, children notice differences in behaviors, play skills and self-help skills of other children. This section was developed to present possible scenarios that parents may find themselves in, and how they can support children learning to understand differences. Young children think in very tangible ways, noticing appearances and behaviors - such as those in wheelchairs, others that have glasses and ones that scream or cry for unknown reasons.

Normally there's no "hidden" agenda to decipher when having a conversation with children. Children tend to say what they think, without understanding that words can be hurtful. They don't understand developmental disabilities or behaviors that they can't see a cause for. Children must learn that everyone is their own person and that we all feel the same emotions. This will help them understand that all people need help, encouragement and respect. It's important to allow children to ask questions about what they see and feel so they learn to become sensitive to the needs of others who are different then themselves.

Parent Interpretation:

What are some situations that you have been in with your child, where they have said something to, or around, another person and you weren't sure what to say in response?

Common Scenarios:

These are some different scenarios that can occur when children are recognizing diversity in others. Below each scenario are suggestions to help parents respond to children's questions and comments in these situations:

1) A child is walking through a playground or public area and sees another child or adult in a wheelchair. The child walks up to the child in the wheelchair and says, "What's that"?

    Appropriate parent response:

    Look at the child and say. "That's a wheelchair. It helps that person move around. They use their wheelchair so they can go places."

    What would you say in this situation?

    What could you say differently, using these tips?

2) A child is in a public place and sees an older person walking with a cane or walker. The child says, "I want to play with that."

    Appropriate parent response:

    "That cane (or walker) helps that person walk. They need a little bit of help to move around. It's not a toy."

    What would you say in this situation?

    What could you say differently, using these tips?

3) A child sees someone with glasses and says, "What are those things on your face?"

    Appropriate parent response:

    "Those are called glasses. They help people's eyes to see better."

    What would you say in this situation?

    What could you say differently, using these tips?

4) A child is walking through the store with their parent when they see another child lying on the floor screaming. The child says, "What's wrong with them? They're really loud."

   Appropriate Parent response:

   "That child seems to be upset about something. Their mommy/daddy is with them helping them feel better. Sometimes when people get upset/angry they need some time to feel better."

   What would you say in this situation?

   What could you say differently, using these tips?

5) A child is playing at the park and they go up to another child playing in the same area. That child runs away or doesn't respond to your child. He/she says, "That little boy/girl won't play with me. They're being mean."

   Appropriate parent response:

   "That little boy/girl may want to play by themselves for a while. It's okay that they want some alone time. Would you like me to play with you?"

   What would you say in this situation?

   What could you say differently, using these tips?

6) A child is playing in an area near other children when another child starts to scream, hit, or throw sand. It doesn't seem like there was anything that caused this behavior. Your child seems scared and unsure of what to do. Your child says, "That little boy/girl is mean. They aren't being nice. I don't want to play with them."

   Appropriate parent response:

   "That little boy/girl seems to be frustrated and I don't know why. They need some time to calm down on their own. Maybe they will be ready to play again in a little while. It's scary sometimes when someone else is screaming and crying, but we all have angry feelings sometimes." Help your child move away from that other child for a while. Allow your child to return and play with that child when the child is ready.

   What would you say in this situation?

   What could you say differently, using these tips?

© JDEducational: Pre-K Your Way: Level 1 Book

Suggested Teaching Activity:

One way to help a child understand that everyone is different is to teach them ways they can support others that may need help. The following activity is something parents can do with their child while they're at home or driving around.

Step 1: Ask the child what they can do.

- Example: "I can: walk/run/jump/swim/hear/see/play/slide, etc."

Step 2: Tell the child you're happy they can do all of those things. They're very lucky. Tell them that some people aren't able to do all those things. Sometimes they need help.

Step 3: Ask the child to think of ways they can help people with different abilities. Tell them to answer the following questions with what they can do to help:

If someone:	Example of Answer:
Has fallen down, I can	Help them get back up
Can't walk, I can	Push their wheelchair
Can't see, I can	Get their glasses for them
Seems angry, I can	Get their mommy to help
Is sad, I can	Give them a hug
Is playing by themselves, I can	Ask them to play with me

Reflection

1) Have you had an experience recently with your child that you weren't sure what to say? How did you respond?

2) Next time this happens, what would be an appropriate response for your child? Keep in mind age appropriate milestones. What words does your child understand? What experiences have they had in the past that would affect the way they respond to this situation?

3) Have you seen other parents react to their children in similar situations? What did you like/dislike about the way they handled the situation?

4) Remember that you have a very hard job! It is not always easy to come up with appropriate responses in a variety of high-stress situations. Are there specific phrases or tips that you learned in this section that will make it easier for you to remember how to respond next time you are in this situation?

5) How could you use the information in this section to support family members who engage with your child when they find themselves in this situation? Would they be open to learning new tips and tricks or not?

6) What are some questions that have come up for you when filling out this section? I would love to hear your questions in our private parenting Facebook group: **JDE Parenting Tips: For Children Under 5**

Putting it into Practice

1) Write down 10 different scenarios where you may use the tips from this section:

Scenario	Your Planned Response (What will you say/do?)	Anticipated Child's Response (How will your child respond?)

2) What will you do if your child doesn't respond the way you anticipated?

Scenario	A way your child might respond (other then the anticipated response from above)	How will you respond?

Conclusion

1) Is there anything else that you would like to learn about this topic?

2) The Following Social/Emotional Learning Objectives are Designed for current Kindergarten Readiness. Circle the ones that you think your child would be able to practice in everyday situations such as those listed above.

- Understanding safety routines.

- Understanding personal care routines.

- Develop self-regulation techniques.

- Acknowledge feelings and appropriate behaviors.

- Understand and identify feelings.

- Understands age appropriate social interactions.

- Communicates through words.

NOTE Section:

....
Thanks for playing!
See you in the next Unit:
Pre-K Your Way - Level 1, Unit 2 Activities

JDEducational
Play · Learn · Grow

JDEducational
Play · Learn · Grow

Pre-K YOUR Way
Level 1 Unit 2

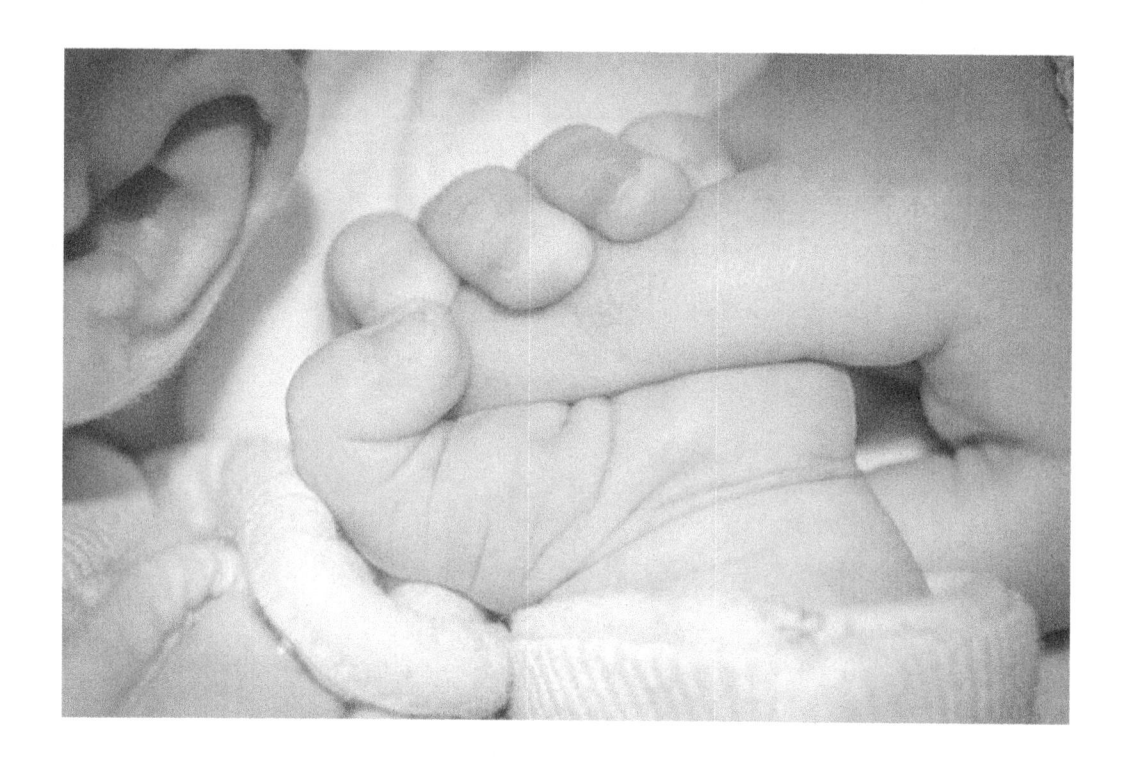

My Family; Taking Turns with Loved Ones

Unit 2: My Family Themed Academic Activities

These activities have been developed to meet specific, age-appropriate, Kindergarten-Readiness skills. These skills are specified in the learning objectives of each activity. The following activities may be completed in any order desired and are specifically designed to address the academic domains: math, science, language, literacy, cognitive, problem solving, and social-emotional development.

Each activity is on its own page. If the adult chooses to print the activities, the space below each activity is provided for adults to write notes regarding the activity. Adults are encouraged to note if the child enjoyed the activity and if the child needs to work on specific learning objectives. Each activity can be repeated more than once to enable the child to master the learning objectives designed for that activity.

Activities

1. My Family Age
2. Family Photo
3. My Family Tree
4. Different vs. Same About
5. Last Name Letters
6. My Family Is
7. Family Match
8. Family Homes
9. Bucket Name
10. Family Pick Up

A1. My Family Age - Activity time: 20 minutes

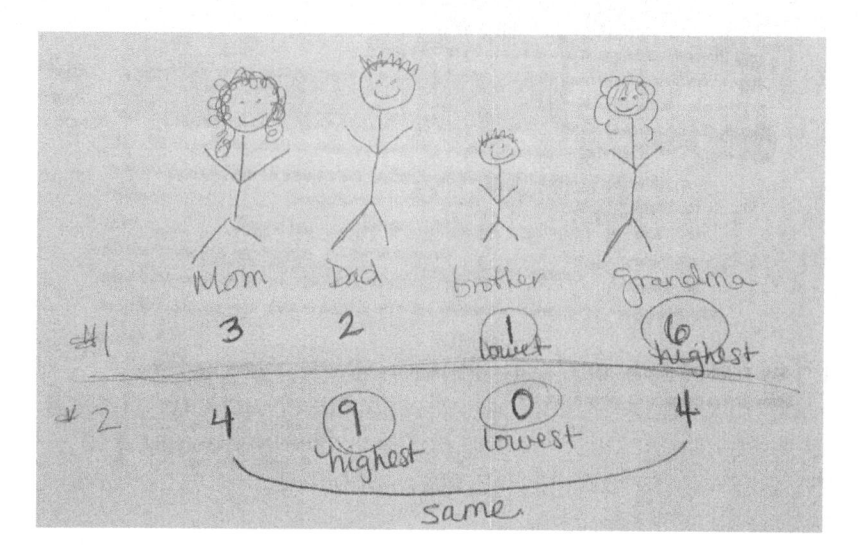

Materials Needed
☐ One (1) Piece of Paper
☐ One (1) Pen
☐ One (1) Box of Crayons

Instructions:

Step 1: Tell your child to use the crayons to draw a picture of every person that lives in their home.

Step 2: Once completed, ask the child to identify who they drew. The adult should label each person in the drawing.

Step 3: Have your child ask each member in the photo how old they are. Help your child wite down the first number of their age.

>For example, Mom is age = **34**, the first number is **3**.

Step 5: The adult should write all the numbers on the child's drawing. See photo above.

Step 6: Ask the child to look at all the numbers. Can they tell which number is smallest? Which number is the largest? **Have the child circle those numbers**.

Step 7: Next, have the child ask each person they drew, what the second number in their age is.

>For example: Age = 3**4**, the second number is **4**

Step 8: The adult should write all of the second numbers **underneath** the first number.

Step 9: Ask the child to look at **all of the second numbers**. Can they tell which number is smallest? Which number is the largest? **Have the child circle those numbers**.

© JDEducational: Pre-K Your Way: Level 1 Book

A.1 Learning Objectives

Math/Science	Language/Literacy	Problem Solving
• Recognize the names of numerals.	• Use words and gestures to communicate.	• Sort objects by one quality (characteristic i.e. Size, color)

Notes: What did your child do well? Are there any skills they need to continue to work on?

A2. Family Photo - Activity time: 20 minute

Materials Needed
- ☐ The picture from Activity A1
- ☐ One (1) Pen
- ☐ One (1) Highlighter
- ☐ One (1) Piece of blank paper

Instructions:

Step 1: Tell the child to look at the picture from Activity A1.

Step 2: The adult should use the pen to write the following words on a blank piece of paper:

- Head
- Eyes
- Nose
- Hands
- Feet
- Fingers

Step 3: Ask the child look at all of the people in the picture.

Step 4: Ask the child how many hands are in the photo. This total includes all of the adults and children's hands they drew. The adult should use the yellow highlighter to write the number next to the corresponding word.

- Head (For example: If there are three people, there would be three heads)
- Eyes (For example: If there are three people, there would be six eyes)
- Nose (For example: If there are three people, there would be three noses)
- Hands (For example: If there are three people, there would be six hands)
- Feet (For example: If there are three people, there would be six feet)
- Fingers (For example: If there are three people, there would be sixty fingers)

Step 5: Ask the child to use a pen to copy the numbers written in yellow highlighter. Can they identify the name each numeral (Example: **3** means **three**)

© JDEducational: Pre-K Your Way: Level 1 Book

A.2 Learning Objectives

Math/Science
- Count up to 5 objects.
- Recognize the names of numerals.

Language/Literacy
- Use words and gestures to communicate.
- Follow new directions.

Problem Solving
- Name body parts and their function.

Notes: What did your child do well? Are there any skills they need to continue to work on?

A3. Family Tree - Activity time: 25 minutes

Materials Needed
- ☐ One (1) printed out photo of everyone in the intermediate and extended family (including parents, grandparents, aunts, uncles and first cousins)

Instructions:

Step 1: The adult should place all the pictures on the floor or table. Tell your child that together, you're going to find out how everyone in your family is related.

Step 2: Ask your child to look through each photo and name the person in each photo.

Step 3: Let's see how everyone is related. Place the photos of grandparents on the table.

Step 4: Place the photos of grandparents children (mom and dad) underneath the photos of the appropriate grandparents.

Step 5: Place the photos of the children underneath their parents.

Example: Place the photo of the paternal grandmother on to the table. Place all of the maternal grandmother's children below the maternal grandmother. **See Example On Next Page..**

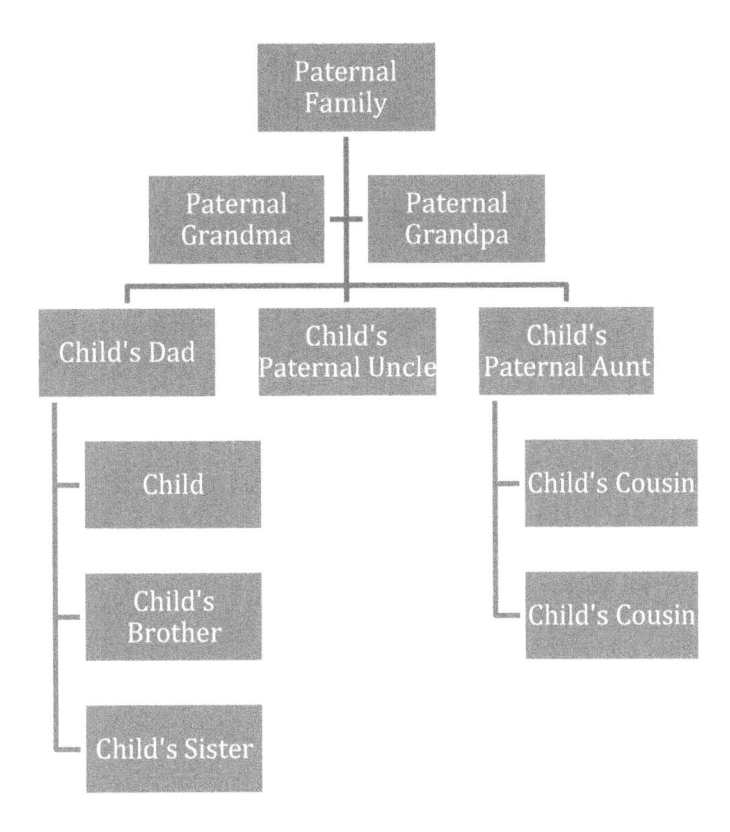

```
                    ┌──────────────┐
                    │  Paternal    │
                    │   Family     │
                    └──────┬───────┘
              ┌────────────┴────────────┐
        ┌─────────────┐          ┌─────────────┐
        │  Paternal   │──────────│  Paternal   │
        │  Grandma    │          │  Grandpa    │
        └─────────────┘          └─────────────┘
   ┌──────────────────────┼──────────────────────┐
┌──────────┐      ┌──────────────┐      ┌──────────────┐
│ Child's  │      │   Child's    │      │   Child's    │
│   Dad    │      │Paternal Uncle│      │Paternal Aunt │
└────┬─────┘      └──────────────┘      └──────┬───────┘
     │                                         │
     ├──[ Child ]                              ├──[ Child's Cousin ]
     │                                         │
     ├──[ Child's Brother ]                    └──[ Child's Cousin ]
     │
     └──[ Child's Sister ]
```

Step 6: Repeat step 5 to include all photos of family members.

Step 7: Ask your child if they can follow the "tree". Have them repeat the following:

"Grandma _____ has (total number of) children. Her children are parent #1, Auntie _____ or Uncle _____, (Parent number 1's siblings). Mommy/Daddy had me, (list all siblings). Auntie/Uncle had my cousins _____(name all cousins)".

Step 8: Repeat Step 5 with all family members from Step 5.

Step 9: Ask your child to point to all of the photos that correspond with the following questions:

1. Who are your grandparents?
2. Who are your cousins?
3. Who are your aunts?
4. Who are your uncles?
5. Who are your brothers?
6. Who are your sisters?

A.3 Learning Objectives

Math/Science	Language/Literacy	Problem Solving
• Count up to 5 objects.	• Use words and gestures to communicate. • Follow New Directions. • Vocabulary Bulding	• Sort objects by characteristic. • Understand Different vs. Same.

Notes: What did your child do well? Are there any skills they need to continue to work on?

A4. Different vs. Same Name - Activity time: 20 minutes

Materials Needed
- ☐ One piece of paper for every member in your immediate family (mom, dad, sisters, brothers and the child).
- ☐ One (1) Box of Crayons
- ☐ One (1) Pen

Instructions:

Step 1: The adult should use a pen to write the first name of **each immediate family member** on the pieces of paper. **One name should be written on each piece of paper**. (See Photo below)

Step 2: Tell the child they're going to look for similarities and differences in the names of their family members.

Step 3: Tell the child to use a crayon to circle the letters that are the same in each name

   (**Example**: Circle all d's with a blue crayon, circle all a's with a green crayon, etc).

Step 4: Ask the child to count all letters that are the same.

Step 5: Ask the child what family members have the same letters that are in the child's first name.

© JDEducational: Pre-K Your Way: Level 1 Book

A.4 Learning Objectives

Math/Science
- N/A

Language/Literacy
- Introduction to written words.
- Introduction to sounds and names of letters.
- Use words and gestures to communicate.

Problem Solving
- Identify three or more colors.
- Understand Different vs. Same.

Notes: What did your child do well? Are there any skills they need to continue to work on?

A5. Last Name Letters - Activity time: 20 minutes

Materials Needed
- ☐ One (1) Piece of Blank Paper
- ☐ One (1) Box of Crayons
- ☐ One (1) Pen
- ☐ One (1) Empty Bucket

Instructions:

Step 1: Tell the child you're going to discover their **last name**. Does the child know what their last name is?

Step 2: The adult should use a pen to write down the child's last name on a piece of blank paper.

Step 3: Ask the child to use any color crayon to trace the letters on the paper.

Step 4: Help the child sound out each letter of their last name.

Step 5: Ask your child to find items throughout their home that **start with each letter** of their last name. Place each item they find into the bucket.

For example: Last name is **SMITH**

1. Items that would go in the bucket:
    - **S** – **S**hirt
    - **M** – **M**agazine
    - **I** – **I**ce Cream Scooper
    - **T** – **T**oothbrush
    - **H** - **H**at

A.5 Learning Objectives

Math/Science	Language/Literacy	Problem Solving
• Name and recognize familiar objects.	• Use words and gestures to communicate. • Identify their own name. • Introduction to Phonological Awareness. • Identify Letters.	• Sort objects by one quality (characteristic i.e. Size, color) • Understand visual symbols.

Notes: What did your child do well? Are there any skills they need to continue to work on?

A6. My Family Is - Activity time: 20 minutes

Materials Needed
- ☐ Two (2) Pieces of Blank Paper
- ☐ One (1) Pen
- ☐ One (1) Box of Crayons

Instructions:

Step 1: Tell your child they're going to write a story about your family.

Step 2: The adult should ask the child the following questions, using a pen to write down their answers on a blank piece of paper.

9. What does your family like to eat for dinner?
10. What does your family like to do at night?
11. What does your family like to do for fun?
12. What does your family like to do for (name a holiday celebration)?
13. What does your family like to do when it is cold outside?
14. What does your family like to do when it is hot outside?

Step 3: Reread your child's answers to them.

Step 4: Encourage the child to use crayons or markers to draw a picture of their family doing something they talked about in Step 2.

A.6 Learning Objectives

Math/Science	Language/Literacy	Problem Solving
• N/A	• Use words and gestures to communicate. • Answer open-ended Questions.	• N/A

Notes: What did your child do well? Are there any skills they need to continue to work on?

A7. Family Match - Activity time: 15 minutes

Materials Needed
- ☐ Pictures from Activity 3
- ☐ The same amount of pieces of blank paper to match the total amount of pictures
- ☐ One (1) Black Marker

Instructions:

Step 1: The adult should use the **black marker** to write **the first names of all the people in the photos.** One name should be written on each piece of paper.

Step 2: Place all the pictures on the floor in a horizontal line.

Step 3: Place the name papers from Step 1 in a horizontal line, 10 feet away from the pictures in Step 2.

Step 4: Have the child pick up one picture from the picture line, then walk over to the lines of paper with written names.

Step 5: The adult should help the child **sound out each letter of that person's name** in the picture the child is holding.

Step 6: Help the child find the piece of paper with the written name that matches the name of the person in the picture the child is holding.

Step 7: The child should place the picture on top of the person's name card.

Step 8: Repeat Steps 4 through 7 until the child has matched all of the pictures to the family member's written names.

A.7 Learning Objectives

Math/Science	Language/Literacy	Problem Solving
• N/A	• Follow New DIrections. • Use words and gestures to communicate. • Introduction to letters. • Phonological Awareness. • Name Identification	• Sort objects by one quality (characteristic i.e. Size, color)

Notes: What did your child do well? Are there any skills they need to continue to work on?

A8. Family Homes - Activity time: 20 minutes

Materials Needed
- ☐ The pieces of paper from Activity 7 of family names written on each piece of paper.
- ☐ A large indoor or outdoor space
- ☐ One (1) Roll of Painters Tape

Instructions:

Step 1: The adult should take all the pieces of paper with family names written on them **from Activity 7 and sort the names into piles** of who lives in the same house.

Step 2: The adult should place the piles of names from Step 1 on the floor. These piles should be placed in order of whose home is the **closest** to the child's home.

For example, see the following diagram:

Pile #1	Pile #2	Pile #3	Pile #4	Pile #5
Child	Aunt	Grandma	Aunt	Grandma
Parent	Uncle	Grandpa	Uncle	Grandpa
Siblings	Cousin		Cousin	
(Where child lives)	(Lives in same city as child)	(Lives in same state as child)	(Lives on the other side of the country)	(Lives in a different country)

© JDEducational: Pre-K Your Way: Level 1 Book

Step 3: The adult should place one short, 12-inch line of painters tape next to each pile. See below:

Pile #1	Pile #2
Child	Aunt
Parent	Uncle
Siblings	Cousin
(Where child lives)	(Lives in same city as child)

Step 4: Tell the child to stand on the taped line next to the pile where they live. This line represents their home.

Step 5: Tell the child they're going to go on **a "trip"** *t*o visit all their family members. First they're going to start with the family that lives **closest to their house**. The trip will end at the home farthest away from their home.

Step 6: Have the child jump from the line under their "home" to the next blue line.

Step 7: Ask the child to look at the pile of names of the people that live in that home. That's the home of family members that live the closet to them. Can they sound out (with help) the names of all the people that live in that home? Who are they and where do they live?

Step 8: Continue jumping to each taped line and repeat Step 7, reminding them that **each "home" they visit is further away from their home.**

Step 9: Once the child identifies the people living in the last home, tell your child that those family members live the **furthest away** from the child's home.

Step 10: Tell the child to turn around and face their "home" (pile with their name on it).

Step 11: Have the child jump back to their home by jumping onto each taped line.

Step 12: Repeat as often as they would like.

© JDEducational: Pre-K Your Way: Level 1 Book

A.8 Learning Objectives

Math/Science	Language/Literacy	Problem Solving
• N/A	• Use words and gestures to communicate. • Follow Multiple-Step Directions. • Introduction to New Vocabulary.	• Sort objects by one quality (characteristic i.e. near vs. far)

Notes: What did your child do well? Are there any skills they need to continue to work on?

A9. Bucket Name - Activity time: 15 minutes

Materials Needed
- ☐ One (1) Piece of Paper with the child's first name written on it.
- ☐ One (1) Empty Bucket
- ☐ One (1) Popsicle stick for each letter in the child's first name) (Example: Jenny would be 5 popsicle sticks)

Instructions:

Step 1: Place the piece of paper on the floor that has the child's name written on it.

Step 2: Place the empty bucket on the floor - three feet away from the child's name.

Step 3: Tell your child to **place one popsicle stick onto each letter of their name (on the paper).**

Step 4: Tell your child to count **how many popsicle sticks there are**. That's how **many letters there are in their name**.

Step 5: Tell your child to stand behind the paper from Step 4, facing the empty bucket.

Step 6: Direct the child to throw each popsicle stick into the empty bucket.

Step 7: Have the child count how many popsicle sticks landed outside of the bucket.

Step 8: Have the child count how many popsicle sticks landed in the bucket.

Step 9: Repeat Steps 5 through 8 as many times as they would like.

A.9 Learning Objectives

Math/Science
- Count up to 5 objects.

Language/Literacy
- Use words and gestures to communicate.
- Letter Identification.
- Name Identification.

Problem Solving
- N/A

Notes: What did your child do well? Are there any skills they need to continue to work on?

A10. Family Pick Up - Activity time: 15 minutes

Materials Needed
- ☐ One (1) Piece of Sidewalk Chalk
- ☐ One Area large enough for the tallest adult to lie down.
- ☐ Printed pictures of the people that live in the child's home
- ☐ Photos from Activity 3

Instructions:

Step 1: Tell the child to lie down on a flat surface.

Step 2: The adult should trace the outline of the child with sidewalk chalk.

Step 3: Next, have each person that lives in the home with the child, lay down next to the child.

Step 4: The child should use the sidewalk chalk to trace the outline of each person.

Step 5: Once everyone has been traced, have them stand up.

Step 6: Tell the child match the person's photo to their outline, using photos from Activity 3. Place the matching photo inside the chalk outline.

Step 7: Next, ask the child if they can find the person **that's the shortest**.

Step 8: Next, ask the child to find the person that's **the tallest.**

Step 9: Have the child pick up and place the photos on the ground in order from the shortest person traced to the tallest person.

Step 10: Now have our child place the photos in order - **from the tallest person to the shortest person.**

A.10 Learning Objectives

Math/Science	Language/Literacy	Problem Solving
• N/A	• Use words and gestures to communicate. • Increase Vocabulary.	• Sort objects by one quality (characteristic i.e. Size, color) • Name body parts and their function.

Notes: What did your child do well? Are there any skills they need to continue to work on?

Behavior Tips – Taking Turns with Loved Ones

Objective:

The purpose of Parenting Tips is to provide ideas and strategies that guide you in supporting your children to reach age appropriate social and emotional milestones. Social and Emotional Milestones include the following:

> **Social/Emotional Development**
>
> - Understanding safety routines.
> - Understanding personal care routines.
> - Develop self-regulation techniques.
> - Acknowledge feelings and appropriate behaviors.
> - Understand and identify feelings.
> - Understands age appropriate social interactions.
> - Communicates through words.

Introduction:

Taking turns and sharing is an advanced social concept for young children to learn. They first have to understand that they will be able to play with the same object at a later time, which means they must understand the concept of time. They also need to understand that although they'll be able to play with that object a later time, they may be asked to share it again. Taking turns requires children to have the foundational social emotional skills in order to to anticipate other people's feelings, such as sad, happy or angry. This is an advanced social concept because children have to detach themselves from their feelings and comprehend another person's feelings, without being upset.

There are different ways to encourage children to share and take turns. Depending on the object, the time of day, and who is requesting to use the object, the child may or may not comply right away. Adults need to understand that it's okay for children to have mixed feelings about sharing. There are things that parents and adults can do to help encourage positive play times and interactions between their child, their siblings and their friends.

Procedures that a parent/adult can put into practice to set up a successful sharing environment:

1) Place a visual timer near the children's play area. If one child would like a turn with an object another child is using, tell them to ask the other child if they can use it for five minutes. Once the child hands the toy over, the adult should set the visual timer to five minutes. When the five-minute bell rings, the child using the item should ask the child who had the item first if they would like the object back.

Examples of Visual Timers:
- Time Timer, sold by School Specialty
- Lakeshore Mini Time Timer, sold by Lakeshore Learning Materials

2) Set up a "Turn List" on the wall for specific "high demand" items. These high demand items can be a new toy one of the children received for a birthday present, a large gross motor toy such as a trampoline or tricycle, or a favorite pool toy.

1. To set up a "Turn List" the parent should take a photo of the item and print it out. The parent should also print a picture of each child present.
2. Place a piece of paper or a clipboard near the desired object.
3. Tape the picture of that object towards the bottom of the clipboard or on the bottom of the piece of paper.
4. When a child wants a turn with the item that another child is using, they can place their photo on the clipboard with the corresponding item on it. This action will signal to the child and the supervising adult that the child, whose picture is on the clipboard, would like to use that object when the current child is finished. Facilitating time limits with certain objects is up to the adult supervising.

Warning: Do not remove an object from a child's hand to place into another child's hand. Doing this may cause the child to feel not only disappointed, but also angry. It's important for children to let go of items themselves. Sometimes an adult will need to get down to the child's level, and enforce taking turns. When this is needed, the adult can help the child come up with a different activity (also known as redirecting the child's attention) to do while they wait for the five-minute timer to go off.

Consistency - make sure to be consistent with turn taking procedures. The more consistent the turn taking routine is, the faster children become more compliant with requests to share.

Scenarios:

Here are some different scenarios that can occur when encouraging children to share. Below each scenario are suggestions for parents on how to respond to children's questions and behaviors in these situations.

Tips to encourage children to share between siblings who are always present:

1. Set up separate play spaces for young children. Each child should be able to have a box of special toys they're not required to share with their sibling(s).
2. Allow a community-play space full of toys and objects where all children are expected to share items in that play space.

Tips to encourage children to share between friends or guests who aren't always present:

1. Tell the child that a new friend will be coming to play with them. If they know the other child, tell them their name.
2. Ask your child to fill up an empty tub with five or six different toys they want to share with or show the child that is visiting.
3. Encourage the child to greet the child that enters the home and guide the guest to the box of toys they would like to share.

Tips to encourage children to share with other adults upon request.

1. Have the adult ask the child for a turn, waiting several seconds before asking again. This will give the child an opportunity to finish what they're doing and process the request from the adult.
2. When the adult is using the object, encourage the adult to talk to the child ("Wow, this yellow crayon is such a pretty color. Thank you for letting me draw my yellow sun with it.")
3. Encourage the adult to return the object to the child within three minutes.

Reflection

1) Have you had an experience recently with your child that you weren't sure what to say? How did you respond?

2) Next time this happens, what would be an appropriate response for your child? Keep in mind age appropriate milestones. What words does your child understand? What experiences have they had in the past that would affect the way they respond to this situation?

3) Have you seen other parents react to their children in similar situations? What did you like/dislike about the way they handled the situation?

4) Remember that you have a very hard job! It is not always easy to come up with appropriate responses in a variety of high-stress situations. Are there specific phrases or tips that you learned in this section that will make it easier for you to remember how to respond next time you are in this situation?

5) How could you use the information in this section to support family members who engage with your child when they find themselves in this situation? Would they be open to learning new tips and tricks or not?

6) What are some questions that have come up for you when filling out this section? I would love to hear your questions in our private parenting Facebook group: **Parenting Tips: Toddler and Preschool Development**

Putting it into Practice

1) Write down 10 different scenarios where you may use the tips from this section:

Scenario	Your Planned Response (What will you say/do?)	Anticipated Child's Response (How will your child respond?)

2) What will you do if your child doesn't respond the way you anticipated?

Scenario	A way your child might respond (other then the anticipated response from above)	How will you respond?

Conclusion

3) Is there anything else that you would like to learn about this topic?

4) The Following Social/Emotional Learning Objectives are Designed for current Kindergarten Readiness. Circle the ones that you think your child would be able to practice in everyday situations such as those listed above.

- Understanding safety routines.

- Understanding personal care routines.

- Develop self-regulation techniques.

- Acknowledge feelings and appropriate behaviors.

- Understand and identify feelings.

- Understands age appropriate social interactions.

- Communicates through words.

NOTE Section:

....
Thanks for playing! See you in the next Unit:
Pre-K Your Way - Level 1, Unit 3 Activities

JDEducational
Play · Learn · Grow

JDEducational
Play · Learn · Grow

Pre-K YOUR Way
Level 1 Unit 3

Literacy Activities;
Teaching Indoor vs. Outdoor Expectations

Unit 3: Learning With Books Themed Academic Activities

These activities have been developed to meet specific, age-appropriate, Kindergarten-Readiness skills. These skills are specified in the learning objectives of each activity. The following activities may be completed in any order desired and are specifically designed to address the academic domains: math, science, language, literacy, cognitive, problem solving, and social-emotional development.

Each activity is on its own page. If the adult chooses to print the activities, the space below each activity is provided for adults to write notes regarding the activity. Adults are encouraged to note if the child enjoyed the activity and if the child needs to work on specific learning objectives. Each activity can be repeated more than once to enable the child to master the learning objectives designed for that activity.

Activities

1. Letter Search
2. Picture Hunt
3. Color Browse
4. Alphabetical
5. Classification
6. How Many
7. Books of Feelings
8. Name Full of Letters
9. My Age in Numbers
10. Spelling My Family

A1. Letter Search - Activity time: 20 minutes

Materials Needed
- ☐ Access to a variety of children's books.
- ☐ One (1) Table or space on the floor where there is enough space for you and your child.
- ☐ One (1) Piece of Paper
- ☐ One (1) Pen

Instructions:

Step 1: The adult and child should sit on the floor surrounded by books. This can be done in your local library or home with your child's books.

Step 2: Ask the child to name **one word**. It can be any word.

Step 3: The adult should use the pen to write down the word the child said on a piece of paper.

Step 4: Tell the child to pick any book they would like to look at.

Step 5: Tell the child you're going to go on a **book letter hunt**.

Step 6: Show the child the word that the adult wrote down on the paper.

Step 7: The adult should tell the child the **name of the first letter**.

Step 8: Ask the child to look through book and see if they can find the same letter.

Step 9: When the child finds that letter in the book, ask the child to use a pen to circle the letter on the piece of paper from Step 7.

Step 10: Help your child identify the name of the **second letter** of the word from Step 6.

Step 11: Have your child repeat Steps 8 through 10 until the child has found all of the letters in the word.

Step 12: Repeat the activity multiple times with new words.

A.1 Learning Objectives

Math/Science	Language/Literacy	Problem Solving
• N/A	• Identify letters. • Phonological Awareness. • Understand that letters make words. • Engage in Literacy Activities.	• Understand Different vs. Same. • Match two items that are the same. • Understand Different vs. Same. • Match two items that are the same.

Notes: What did your child do well? Are there any skills they need to continue to work on?

A2. Picture Hunt - Activity time: 20 minutes

Materials Needed
- ☐ Access to a variety of children's books.
- ☐ One (1) Table or space on the floor that a child can place up to 5 books.
- ☐ One (1) Piece of Paper
- ☐ One (1) Pen

Instructions:

Step 1: The adult and child should sit on the floor surrounded by books. This can be done in your local library or home with your child's books.

Step 2: The adult should ask the child the child the following questions and use a pen to write down their responses:

1. What is your favorite animal?
2. What is your favorite food?
3. What is your favorite place? (Example: beach, park).

The adult can come up with two more questions regarding something else that's their favorite.

Step 3: Tell the child you're going to read of the words they said. Their job is to find a book that has a picture of the item they said.

Step 4: Tell the child what they said their **favorite animal** is. Tell the child find a book with the picture of that animal in it.

Step 5: When your child finds it, have them show the adult the picture then put the book back where they found it.

Step 6: Repeat steps 3 through 5 until the child finds all the pictures that match the answers they gave in Step 2.

Step 7: It's the adult's turn to answer the questions in Step 2. Tell the child what the adult's favorite animal is.

Step 8: Ask the child to look through books to find that animal and show it to the adult.

Step 9: Repeat steps 7 and 8 until the child finds all the pictures that match the adult's answers they gave in Step 2.

Step 10: Repeat with new questions such as: What is your least favorite _____?

A.1 Learning Objectives

Math/Science	Language/Literacy	Problem Solving
• N/A	• Engage in Literacy Activities.	• Match words to pictures. • Understand Different vs. Same.

Notes: What did your child do well? Are there any skills they need to continue to work on?

A3. Color Browse - Activity time: 15 minutes

Materials Needed
- ☐ Access to a variety of children's books.
- ☐ One (1) Box of Crayons

Instructions:

Step 1: The adult and child should sit on the floor or at a table surrounded by books. This can be done in your local library or home with your child's books.

Step 2: Tell the child they're going to find **one book** to **match each crayon color** in the crayon box.

Step 3: The adult should pick out one crayon from the crayon box and ask the child:

- "What color is this?"

Step 4: Ask the child find a book that has the same color on the cover.

Step 5: When the child finds it, have them point to the color on the cover, name the color and then put the book back.

Step 6: Continue Steps 3 through 5 until the child matches all of the colors from the crayon box.

A.3 Learning Objectives

Math/Science	Language/Literacy	Problem Solving
•N/A	•Engage in Literacy Activities. •Increase Vocabulary	•Match colors. •Understand Different vs. Same.

Notes: What did your child do well? Are there any skills they need to continue to work on?

A4. Alphabetical - Activity time: 30 minutes

Materials Needed
- ☐ Access to a variety of children's books.
- ☐ One (1) Pen
- ☐ Twenty-Six (26) Blank 3x5 index cards (any color)
- ☐ One (1) Blank Piece of Paper

Instructions:

Step 1: – The adult should write **letters A through Z**, one letter on each index card.

Step 2: The adult and child should sit on the floor or at a table surrounded by books. This can be done in your local library or home with your child's books.

Step 3: Show the child one 3x5 index card with any letter on it. Help the child name the letter on the card.

Step 4: Give the child the 3x5 index card and tell them to find a book whose title has the same letter in it. The child can carry the 3x5 index card around as a reference.

Step 5: When the child brings the book back, ask them to place the matching 3x5 letter index card on top of the book.

Step 6: Continue Step 3 through step 5 until the child finds a book with each letter of the alphabet.

Step 7: Help the child place the books in alphabetical order, based on the 3x5 index cards. (The book the child found that has the letter A in it should be first in line. The book with the letter B goes next, and so on).

Step 8: Once all of the books are in a line, ask the child count **how many books** there are. There are **26 books and 26 letters** of the alphabet.

Step 9: The adult should write the **child's name** on a blank piece of paper.

Step 10: Ask your child to spell their name with the books by making a new row with the books that match letters that match their name (the books with the index cards on them that match the letters in their name).

Step 11: Ask the child to organize the books from Step 10 in the order of their name.

Step 12: Encourage the child to pick one of the books in Step 11 to read.

Step 13: Now it's time to put the books back where they belong.

A.4 Learning Objectives

Math/Science	Language/Literacy	Problem Solving
• Counting - One to One Correspondance. (1 through 26)	• Engage in Literacy Activities. • Increase Vocabulary. • Letter identification. • Name Identification. • Understand that letters make words. • Follow simple directions.	• Match objects by one trait. • Understand Different vs. Same. • Introduction to visual representation

Notes: What did your child do well? Are there any skills they need to continue to work on?

© JDEducational: Pre-K Your Way: Level 1 Book

A5. Classification - Activity time: 20 minutes

> **Materials Needed**
> ☐ Access to a variety of children's books.
> ☐ Five (5) books with cars on the cover
> ☐ Five (5) books with animals on the cover
> ☐ Five (5) books with food on the cover

Instructions:

Step 1: The adult and child should sit on the floor or at a table surrounded by books. This can be done in your local library or home with your child's books.

Step 2: The adult should find the books listed in the materials list.

Step 3: The adult should mix all of the books up and then place them in front of the child.

Step 4: Tell the child to sort the books into the following three categories (the adult can place once book of each category in a separate pile and the child can finish):

- Food
- Animals
- Cars

Step 5: Tell the child to use the same books to sort by the following characteristics (the adult can place once book of each category in a separate pile and the child can finish):

1. By First Letter in the Title
2. By Colors on the Cover
3. By Paperback vs. Hardcover books.

Step 6: The adult can pick three new book categories and repeat step 4 and 5.

A.5 Learning Objectives

Math/Science
- Counting - One through Five

Language/Literacy
- Engage in Literacy Activities.
- Increase Vocabulary.
- Letter identification.
- Picture Identification.
- Follow simple directions.

Problem Solving
- Match objects by one characteristic.
- Understand Different vs. Same.
- Identify three or more colors.

Notes: What did your child do well? Are there any skills they need to continue to work on?

A6. How Many - Activity time: 20 minutes

Materials Needed
☐ Access to a variety of children's books.
☐ Ten (10) Children's books
☐ Ten (10) Sticky Notes or Small pieces of paper
☐ One (1) Pen

Instructions:

Step 1: The adult should place **ten children's books** on a table or on the floor in front of the child.

Step 2: Ask the child pick one book out of the pile from Step 1.

Step 3: Ask the child to look through the book and count how many pages are in that book. When the child opens the book, the picture on the left counts as page one.

Step 4: Is there a **Numeral** written on the last page that states **how many pages** there are in the book? If so, tell the child what number that numeral represents.

Step 5: Once the child discovers how many pages there are in one book, the adult should write the number on a sticky note (or small piece of paper) and place it on the cover of the book.

Step 6: Have the child repeat Step 2 through Step 5 with the remaining books in the pile.

Step 7: Ask the child to look at all the numbers on the sticky notes. Tell them to place the books with the **same amount of pages** into a pile together.

Step 8: Ask the child to count how many books are in each pile.

Step 9: Time to put the books away.

A.6 Learning Objectives

Math/Science
- Count up to 5 objects.
- Recognize the names of numerals.

Language/Literacy
- Use words and gestures to communicate.
- Engage in Literacy Activities.
- Increase Vocabulary.

Problem Solving
- Sort objects by one quality (characteristic i.e. Size, color)
- Understand Different vs. Same.

Notes: What did your child do well? Are there any skills they need to continue to work on?

A7. Books of Feelings - Activity time: 15 minutes

Materials Needed
☐ Access to a variety of children's books.

Instructions:

Step 1: The adult and child should sit on the floor or at a table surrounded by books. This can be done in your local library or home with your child's books.

Step 2: Tell the child they're going to **play a feelings game**. Ask the child to name a feeling.

Step 3: Tell the child to look for children's books that have picture of a character in a book who matches that feeling.

For example: If the child picks **"happy"**, the child can look in any children's book for any character that is **smiling or laughing.**

Step 4: Repeat Step 3 with the following feelings:

List of feelings:
1. Happy
2. Sad
3. Mad
4. Laughing
5. Tired
6. Sleepy
7. Excited
8. Angry

Step 5: Tell the child to put the books back.

Step 6: Can the child think of any more feelings they want to find.

A.7 Learning Objectives

Math/Science	Language/Literacy	Problem Solving
• N/A	• Use words and gestures to communicate. • Engage in Literacy Activities. • Increase Vocabulary. • Demonstrate awareness of the feelings of others.	• Sort objects by one quality (characteristic i.e. Size, color) • Understand Different vs. Same.

Notes: What did your child do well? Are there any skills they need to continue to work on?

A8. Name Full of Letters - Activity time: 15 minutes

Materials Needed
- ☐ Access to a variety of children's books.
- ☐ One (1) Pen
- ☐ One (1) Blank Piece of Paper

Instructions:

Step 1: The adult and child should sit on the floor or at a table surrounded by books. This can be done in your local library or home with your child's books.

Step 2: The adult should write the child's name on the piece of paper.

Step 3: Tell the child to look at all the titles of the children's books. The title are the words on the front of the books.

Step 4: Show the child the piece of paper with their name on it.

Step 5: Ask them to find one book for each letter of their name.

Step 6: Once the child finds all the letters in their name, using the titles of different books, have the child place the books in the order that represents the letters in their name.

Step 7: Read all of the books in order, starting with the book that has the first letter of their name, ending with the book that has the last letter in their name. When moving onto the next book, have the child find the letter that is in their name on the page.

Step 8: Ask your child to sound out the first letter in their name. Can they come up with a title of a new book that starts with the first letter of their name?

Example:

Child's name – **S**ara
Book Title – **S**oothing Sammy

Step 9: Ask your child to sound out to repeat step 8 for the rest of the letters in their first name?

Example:

Child's name – **S**ara
Book Title – **A**pple Pie Day

Step 10: Tell your child that they also have a last name.

Step 11: Write their last name on a piece of paper.

Step 12: Repeat steps 4 through 9 with their child's last name.

Step 13: Now it's time to put the books back where they came from.

A.8 Learning Objectives

Math/Science	Language/Literacy	Problem Solving
• N/A	• Use words and gestures to communicate. • Engage in Literacy Activities. • Identify names of letters. • Identify sounds of letters (phonological awareness). • Vocabulary Development.	• Sort objects by one quality (characteristic i.e. Size, color) • Understand Different vs. Same.

Notes: What did your child do well? Are there any skills they need to continue to work on?

© JDEducational: Pre-K Your Way: Level 1 Book

A9. My Age in Numbers - Activity time: 15 minutes

Materials Needed
- ☐ Access to a variety of children's books.
- ☐ One (1) Pen
- ☐ One (1) Piece of paper

Instructions:

Step 1: The adult and child should sit on the floor or at a table surrounded by books. This can be done in your local library or home with your child's books.

Step 2: Ask the child:

- "How old are you?"

Step 3: The adult should write down the **numeral that matches that child's age**.

Example: If the child is three years old, the adult should write down "3" on a piece of paper.

Step 4: Tell the child to look for **five books** that have **the number in the book** which matches their age.

Step 5: Once the child **finds 5 books**, have them show the adult **where the number is located** in the book.

Step 6: The adult and child can read the books that the child found.

Step 7: Make sure to put all the books away.

© JDEducational: Pre-K Your Way: Level 1 Book

A.9 Learning Objectives

Math/Science
- Count up to 5 objects.
- Recognize the names of numerals.

Language/Literacy
- Use words and gestures to communicate.
- Engage in Literacy Activities.
- Increase Vocabulary.

Problem Solving
- Sort objects by one quality (characteristic i.e. Size, color)
- Understand Different vs. Same.

Notes: What did your child do well? Are there any skills they need to continue to work on?

A10. Spelling My Family - Activity time: 15 minutes

Materials Needed
- ☐ Access to a variety of children's books.
- ☐ One (1) Pen
- ☐ One (1) Piece of paper

Instructions:

Step 1: The adult and child should sit on the floor or at a table surrounded by books. This can be done in your local library or home with your child's books.

Step 2: Ask the child: "Who lives at home with you?" Make sure they remember to list all the people and animals that live at home with them.

Step 3: Write down what the child says on a blank piece of paper.

Step 4: Ask the child to count **how many boys are listed.**

Step 5: The adult should write down the number of boys there are.

Step 6: Repeat Step 3 and Step 4 for counting the **amount of girls there are**.

Step 7: Next, encourage the child to count **how many animals are listed**.

Step 8: The adult should write down the **type and amount** of each animal the child says.

Step 9: Tell the child to go find one book that has a picture representing each family member on the cover.

For example: If there are 2 girls, 1 boy, 1 dog and 1 fish that live in their home, child should find:

- two books, each with one girl on the cover.
- one book that has one boy on the cover.
- one book that has one dog on the cover.
- one book that has one fish on the cover.

© JDEducational: Pre-K Your Way: Level 1 Book

Step 10: When the child brings back each book, the adult should ask the child to point out which picture represents each person in their family? For example: "Which girl is the mommy?" etc.

Step 11: Time to put the books away.

> **Take it to the Next Level:** Ask the child to find characters in books that represent extended family members, neighbors and friends.

A.10 Learning Objectives

Math/Science	Language/Literacy	Problem Solving
• N/A	• Use words and gestures to communicate. • Engage in Literacy Activities. • Increase Vocabulary.	• Sort objects by one quality (characteristic i.e. Size, color) • Understand Different vs. Same.

Notes: What did your child do well? Are there any skills they need to continue to work on?

Behavior Tips – Understanding Indoor vs. Outdoor Expectations

The purpose of Parenting Tips is to provide ideas and strategies that guide you in supporting your children to reach age appropriate social and emotional milestones. Social and Emotional Milestones include the following:

> **Social/Emotional Development**
> - Understanding safety routines.
> - Understanding personal care routines.
> - Develop self-regulation techniques.
> - Acknowledge feelings and appropriate behaviors.
> - Understand and identify feelings.
> - Understands age appropriate social interactions.
> - Communicates through words.

Order of Operation: Read through the tips and suggestions that correspond with the identified behavior. At your own pace, work through the questions in the worksheet area at the end of this section.

> **Objective:**
>
> What are the age-appropriate rules and expectations regarding appropriate behaviors in different environments.

Introduction:

When children are happy or excited, they express their feelings through actions and their voice. When a child is happy they may laugh, run or gallop. When a child is mad they may scream, cry or knock something over. It doesn't matter where the child is, they will express their emotions, sometimes demonstrating behaviors that are inappropriate for the environment they're in.

In order for children to understand and follow through on behavior expectations, rules and expectations need to be discussed in an age appropriate manner, which includes, simple and short directions combined with visual and verbal cues. Children require behavior expectations to be explained to them before they enter into an environment, and frequently thereafter. Consistency and follow through are the most important aspects of working with young children. Rules and expectations for individual environments should always stay the same. A child will become confused if an adult allows a child to be loud when visiting a specific place, and during the next visit, the adult expects the child to stay quiet. This will lead to the child forgetting the current behavior expectations, resulting in parent frustration.

Suggestions on how to teach children expectations for a quiet environment (such as a library or office):
- Tell your child you're going to go to a place where only whisper voices are allowed.
- Tell your child that if they need to move and wiggle, they can tell the adult and they can take a break from that space.
- Tell your child that there will be other people in that location that will be working and need to have quiet so they can concentrate.
- Make sure that the adult has plenty of quiet activities for the child to do (color crayons and books, building blocks, books to read)
- Every 45 minutes, remove the child from that environment for 10 to 15 minutes so they can talk and run.
- Make sure the child has plenty of water and snacks so they feel comfortable.

Suggestions on how to teach children the expectation for a loud and energetic environment (such as a park):
- Tell the child you're going to a place where there will be a lot of noise and people talking and moving around.
- Tell the child the expectations of where they should be. For example, if you're going to a park, tell the child that they need to stay in the sand area and stay where they can see you and you can see them.
- Make sure the child knows that if the environment gets too loud or there are too many people, it's okay if they check in with the adult and take a break.

- If it's too loud for the child and they would like a break, the adult and child can go sit in a car or sit in an area away from the noise for five or ten minutes.
- Make sure the child has plenty of water and snacks so they feel comfortable.

Suggestions on helping a child go to a place/activity that is new and has a lot of rules (such as grandma's house for Thanksgiving Dinner):

- Tell the child where you're going and what you're going to do there. (We are going to grandma's house. We are going to eat dinner there.)
- Tell your child if there are any new rules. (When we get there, you can play with your cousins, Jenny and Sarah, but make sure you don't go into grandma's bedroom because she doesn't want anyone playing in there).
- When you get to the location, walk your child around the area so they feel comfortable and show them what they're going to do. (We're at grandma's house. There are a lot of people. See this blue high chair. This is where you are going to sit, right next to mommy, when it's dinnertime tonight).
- Make sure the adult checks in with the child frequently throughout the event.

Step by Step Guide for Preparing for a Community Outing:

1) Where are you going? _____

2) What is the noise expectation? _____

3) What do I have with me to keep my child entertained during this outing?

   a. _____

   b. _____

   c. _____

4) Will I be gone during lunch or snack time?

   a. If yes, what snacks/drinks do I have?

   _____

5) Will I be gone during nap time?

   a. If yes, what types of quiet time activities do I have?

   _____

   b. What type of comforting items have I brought (favorite stuffed animal/blanket/book/cup)

_____

6) Have I told my child what to expect?

7) Have I prepared my child on how long this outing will be and with whom?

8) Do I have a plan on where I can take my child if they need a break?

Reflection

1) Have you had an experience recently with your child that you weren't sure what to say? How did you respond?

2) Next time this happens, what would be an appropriate response for your child? Keep in mind age appropriate milestones. What words does your child understand? What experiences have they had in the past that would affect the way they respond to this situation?

3) Have you seen other parents react to their children in similar situations? What did you like/dislike about the way they handled the situation?

4) Remember that you have a very hard job! It is not always easy to come up with appropriate responses in a variety of high-stress situations. Are there specific phrases or tips that you learned in this section that will make it easier for you to remember how to respond next time you are in this situation?

5) How could you use the information in this section to support family members who engage with your child when they find themselves in this situation? Would they be open to learning new tips and tricks or not?

6) What are some questions that have come up for you when filling out this section? I would love to hear your questions in our private parenting Facebook group: JDE Parenting Tips: For Children Under 5

Putting it into Practice

1) Write down 10 different scenarios where you may use the tips from this section:

Scenario	Your Planned Response (What will you say/do?)	Anticipated Child's Response (How will your child respond?)

2) What will you do if your child doesn't respond the way you anticipated?

Scenario	A way your child might respond (other then the anticipated response from above)	How will you respond?

Conclusion

5) Is there anything else that you would like to learn about this topic?

6) The Following Social/Emotional Learning Objectives are Designed for current Kindergarten Readiness. Circle the ones that you think your child would be able to practice in everyday situations such as those listed above.

   i. Understanding safety routines.

   ii. Understanding personal care routines.

   iii. Develop self-regulation techniques.

   iv. Acknowledge feelings and appropriate behaviors.

   v. Understand and identify feelings.

   vi. Understands age appropriate social interactions.

   vii. Communicates through words.

NOTE Section:

Thanks for playing! See you in the next Unit:
Level 1, Unit 4 Activities

JDEducational
Play · Learn · Grow

JDEducational
Play · Learn · Grow

Pre-K YOUR Way
Level 1 Unit 4

Discovering My Five Senses;
Supporting Age Appropriate Behavior

Unit 4: Discovering My 5 Senses Activities

These activities have been developed to meet specific, age-appropriate, Kindergarten-Readiness skills. These skills are specified in the learning objectives of each activity. The following activities may be completed in any order desired and are specifically designed to address the academic domains: math, science, language, literacy, cognitive, problem solving, and social-emotional development.

Each activity is on its own page. If the adult chooses to print the activities, the space below each activity is provided for adults to write notes regarding the activity. Adults are encouraged to note if the child enjoyed the activity and if the child needs to work on specific learning objectives. Each activity can be repeated more than once to enable the child to master the learning objectives designed for that activity.

1. Texture Sort
2. Tasting Colors
3. Hearing Voices
4. Smelling my World
5. Seeing Opposites
6. Matching Sounds
7. Color My Voice
8. Music Maker
9. Toe, Touch, Feel
10. See My Way

A1. Texture Sort - Activity time: 20 minutes

Materials Needed
- ☐ Three (3) Items that are soft (i.e. blanket, stuffed animal, pillow)
- ☐ Three (3) Items that are hard (i.e. book, plastic toy, cookie sheet)

Instructions:

Step 1: The adult should gather the items listed in the "materials needed" section for this activity. Place those items on the floor in front of the child.

Step 2: Ask the child to touch all the items with their hands.

Step 3: Ask the child to touch all the items with their feet.

Step 4: Ask the child to describe what the objects feel like.

Step 5: Tell the child that some of these items **are "hard"** and some of the items **are "soft"**.

Step 6: Next, the adult should ask the child to sort the items by how the feel:

- Place the soft items in one pile.
- Place the hard items in a separate pile.

Step 7: Tell the child the objects in the two piles feel very different from each other.

> **Take it to the Next Level:** Ask your child to go on a hunt around the house to find other object that feel the same.
>
> For example:
>
> - Items that are squishy
> - Items that are bumpy
> - Items that are scratchy
> - Items that are cold

© JDEducational: Pre-K Your Way: Level 1 Book

A.1 Learning Objectives

Math/Science	Language/Literacy	Problem Solving
• N/A	• Understand rules and expectations. • Follow unfamiliar directions. • Use words and gestures to communicate. • Build Vocabulary.	• Sort objects by one quality (characteristic i.e. Size, color) • Understand Different vs. Same. • Classify objects by at least two properties.

Notes: What did your child do well? Are there any skills they need to continue to work on?

A2. Tasting Colors - Activity time: 20 minutes

Materials Needed
- ☐ Five (4) Plastic, see through cups
- ☐ One (1) Packet of food color (with at least four colors)
- ☐ One (1) 8 ounce cup of water

Instructions:

Step 1: The adult should place the four cups on a flat surface.

Step 2: The adult should pour two ounces of water into each cup.

Step 3: The adult should place **three drops** of food coloring - **one color** in each cup.

> **Example:**
> - **Three drops of** blue in the first cup
> - **Three drops of** red in the second cup
> - **Three drops of**   in the third cup and green in the fourth cup.

Step 4: Ask the child to name each color.

Step 5: Tell the child that each of these cups is filled with colored water.

Step 6: Ask the child: "Do the colors taste different?"

Step 7: Ask the child to **find one item** around them **that is the same color** as each watercolor.

Step 8: Tell the child to **place each colored** item **next to the matching colored water**.

Step 9: Allow the child to taste each color.

Step 10: Ask the child if the colors (water) taste different or the same.

A.2 Learning Objectives

Math/Science
- Understand different parts of the body and their functions.

Language/Literacy
- Participate in familiar routines.
- Understand rules and expectations.
- Follow Unfamiliar Directions.
- Use words and gestures to communicate.

Problem Solving
- Identify three or more colors.
- Sort objects by one quality (characteristic i.e. Size, color)

Notes: What did your child do well? Are there any skills they need to continue to work on?

A3. Hearing Voices - Activity time: 15 minutes

Materials Needed
- ☐ One electronic device that can record sound (i.e. Cell phone)

Instructions:

Step 1: The adult should record the voices of each family member, neighbor and friend that your child interacts with on a daily basis. Have each person say **"Hello (child's name)"**.

**Make sure each person records their own segment, with no overlapping voices.

Step 2: Sit with the child and tell them **they're going to use their ears to listen**.

Step 3: The adult should play each person's recording, one at a time. After each recording, ask the child if they can guess whose voice they heard.

Step 4: The adult can replay each recording until the child is able to guess who is speaking.

Take it to the Next Level: If there are pets that live in the home, the adult can record the animals "speaking" (i.e. the dog barking).

A.3 Learning Objectives

Math/Science	Language/Literacy	Problem Solving
• Understand different parts of the body and their functions.	• Use words and gestures to communicate.	• Identify object, people or places by sound. • Introduction to Audiory Cues.

Notes: What did your child do well? Are there any skills they need to continue to work on?

A4. Smelling My World - Activity time: 20 minutes

Materials Needed
- ☐ One (1) Pen
- ☐ Two (2) Pieces of paper
- ☐ One (1) Clove of Garlic
- ☐ One (1) Lemon
- ☐ One (1) Orange
- ☐ One (1) Basil Leaf
- ☐ One (1) Mint Leaves
- ☐ Five (5) Small Paper or Plastic Cups

Instructions:

Step 1: Tell the child they're going to do a smell test.

Step 2: The adult should use the pen to write "Like" on top of one piece of paper and "Don't Like" on top of the second piece of paper.

Like	Don't Like

Step 3: The adult should put ½ **Clove of Garlic, crushed,** in one small paper cup.

Step 4: The adult should put **1 slice of Orange** in another small paper cup.

Step 5: The adult should put **1 slice of Lemon** in another small paper cup.

Step 6: The adult should put **1 Basil leaf** in another small paper cup.

Step 7: The adult should put **1 Mint leaf** in another small paper cup.

Step 8: Place the cup with crushed garlic in front of the child.

Step 9: Ask the child to smell the garlic.

Step 10: Ask the child if they like the smell or "don't like" the smell.

Step 11: The adult should **write the word "garlic"** on the piece of paper that says "like", if the child likes the smell OR the adult should write the word "garlic" on the piece of paper that says "don't like," if the child didn't like the smell.

Step 12: Repeat step 8 through step 11 with the rest of the cups of items.

Step 13: Ask the child to count how many "smells" that are written on the "like" list.

Step 14: The adult should write the numeral that represents that number on the "like" list (Example: three smells = 3).

Like

Orange
Mint
Lemon

3

Step 15: Ask the child to count how many "smells" that are written on the "don't like" list.

Step 16: The adult should write the numeral that represents that number on the "don't like" list (Example: two smells = 2).

Don't Like

Garlic
Mint

2

Step 17: The adult should ask the child which list had more, the "like" list or the "don't like" list?

A.4 Learning Objectives

Math/Science
- Count up to 5 objects.
- Recognize the names of numerals.
- Understand different parts of the body and their functions.

Language/Literacy
- Use words and gestures to communicate.
- Build Vocabulary.

Problem Solving
- Sort objects by one quality (characteristic i.e. Size, color)
- Classify objects

Notes: What did your child do well? Are there any skills they need to continue to work on?

A5. Seeing Opposites - Activity time: 20 minutes

Materials Needed
- ☐ Two (2) Items: One item that is at least 2 feet long.
- ☐ One item that is 1 foot long, or smaller

Instructions:

Step 1: Tell the child they're going to **see "Opposites"**.

Step 2: The adult should place the two objects from the materials list in front of the child. Ask the child to look at the objects with their eyes. That is how they see.

Step 3: Ask the child to name, or point, to the object that is **bigger.**

Step 4: Ask the child to name, or point, to the object that is **smaller.**

Step 5: Next, the adult should place one of the objects **in front of the child** and **one of the objects two feet away** from the child.

Step 6: Ask the child if they can name, or point, to the object that is **closer.**

Step 7: Ask the child if they can name, or point, to the object that is **father.**

Step 8: Next, the adult should place one of the objects **on the floor** and one of the objects **on top of a piece of furniture.**

Step 9: Ask the child if they can name, or point, to the object that is **Lower/Down.**

Step 10: Ask the child if they can name, or point, to the object that is **Higher/Up.**

Step 11: Tell the child our eyes are used to help us see and tell our bodies where objects around us are. That way we don't walk into objects.

© JDEducational: Pre-K Your Way: Level 1 Book

A.5 Learning Objectives

Math/Science
- Understand different parts of the body and their functions.

Language/Literacy
- Use words and gestures to communicate.
- Build Vocabulary.
- Answer simple questions.

Problem Solving
- Identify object by positional words.

Notes: What did your child do well? Are there any skills they need to continue to work on?

A6. Matching Sounds - Activity time: 10 minutes

Materials Needed
- ☐ Six (6) Empty Plastic eggs (any colors)
- ☐ Four (4) Pennies
- ☐ Two (2) Tablespoons of Rice

Instructions:

Step 1: The adult should pick two plastic eggs (any color) and close them, putting nothing inside.

Step 2: The adult should pick two plastic eggs (any color) and put two pennies in each egg. Close the eggs. If needed, tape them shut.

Step 3: The adult should pick two plastic eggs (any color) and put one tablespoon of rice in each egg. Close the eggs. If needed, tape them shut.

Step 4: Have the child gather the eggs and place the eggs next to each other on the ground.

Step 5: Tell the child they're going to use their ears to find out which eggs sound the same.

Step 6: Allow the child to shake each egg. Tell them to shake it **five times**

- Can they pick out the three sets of eggs that have the same objects in them, based on their sounds?
- Which eggs have rice?
- Which eggs have pennies?
- Which eggs have nothing in it?
- Which eggs sound the same?

A.6 Learning Objectives

Math/Science
- Understand Body Parts and their Function.
- Count up to 5 objects.

Language/Literacy
- Use words and gestures to communicate with same aged peers.
- Follow unfamiliar directions.

Problem Solving
- Sort objects by one quality (characteristic i.e. Size, color)
- Understand Different vs. Same.

Notes: What did your child do well? Are there any skills they need to continue to work on?

A7. Color My Voice - Activity time: 15 minutes

Materials Needed
- ☐ One (1) Piece of Paper
- ☐ One (1) Box of Crayons

Instructions:

Step 1: The adult should sit with the child near a hard surface that the child can use to draw a picture on.

Step 2: Ask the child to choose a crayon from the crayon box.

Step 3: Tell the child the adult is going to make some sounds. They should do the following:

1. When the adult **starts to make a sound**, the child should start to **draw a line or squiggle.**
2. When the adult **stops making the sound** the child should **stop drawing** and put the crayon down.

Step 4: The adult should saying the sound **"laaaaaaaaa" for three seconds.**

1. As soon as the adult starts to say **"laa"** the child should start drawing a line or squiggle.
2. After **3 seconds** stop saying **"laaa"**. The child should stop drawing immediately.

Step 5: Tell the child to **pick a new crayon color**. The adult should say the sound **"moooooooo" for five seconds.**

1. As soon as the adult starts to say, **"moo"** the child **should start drawing a line or squiggle**.
2. After **5 seconds** stop saying **"moo"**. The child should stop drawing immediately.

Step 6: Tell the child to pick a new crayon color. The adult should say the sound **"grrrrrrrrrr" for ten seconds.**

1. As soon as the adult starts to say, **"grr"** the child **should start drawing a line or squiggle**.

2. After **10 seconds** stop saying **"grr"**. The child should stop drawing immediately.

Step 7: Tell the child to pick a new crayon color. The adult should say the sound **"eeeeeeeeeeeee" for 20 seconds.**

1. As soon as the adult starts to say, **"eee"** the child **should start drawing a line or squiggle**.

2. After **20 seconds** stop saying **"eee"**. The child should stop drawing immediately.

Step 8: Ask the child to look at all of the lines or squiggles they drew. Ask the child:

- Which line is the longest? Why? What color is it?
- Which line is the shortest? Why? What color is it?

A.7 Learning Objectives

Math/Science	Language/Literacy	Problem Solving
• Introduction to Measurement.	• Use words and gestures to communicate. • Follow simple directions.	• Identify three or more colors. • Identify objects by one quality (characteristic i.e. Size, color)

Notes: What did your child do well? Are there any skills they need to continue to work on?

A8. Music Maker - Activity time: 20 minutes

Materials Needed
- ☐ A large indoor or outdoor space where your child can move around on the ground safely. The ground should be hard, so if the child stomps it will make noise (sounds).

Instructions:

Step 1: Tell the child they're going to make some music.

Step 2: Tell the child to use their feet to stomp on the ground two times.

Step 3: Tell the child to clap their hands five times.

Step 4: Tell the child to click their tongue three times.

Step 5: The adult should tell the child to repeat Step 2 through Step 4 at a faster pace.

Step 6: The adult should tell the child to repeat Step 2 through Step 4 as fast as they can.

Step 7: Congratulations! They just made music with their body.

Take it to the Next Level: Can the child come up with more ways to make new sounds? (Example: Whistle, snapping fingers or smacking their lips together).

A.8 Learning Objectives

Math/Science	Language/Literacy	Problem Solving
• Count up to 5 objects.	• Follow unfamiliar directions. • Use words and gestures to communicate.	• N/A

Notes: What did your child do well? Are there any skills they need to continue to work on?

A9. Toe, Touch, Feel - Activity time: 15 minutes

Materials Needed
- ☐ One (1) Bucket of Water (the water should be less than 2 inches deep)
- ☐ One (1) Hard Surface to place the bucket of water on.

Instructions:

Step 1: Tell the child they're going to do a toe pattern dance. They're going to feel wet and dry.

Step 2: Tell the child to place their big toe in the bucket of water, and then put in on the dry ground. This is called a toe water tap.

Step 3: Tell the child the following directions:

- When the adult says "wet" the child should touch the water with their toe.
- When the adult days "dry" the child should tap the same toe on the ground.

Step 4: The adult should say the following patterns:

1. Wet, Wet, Dry, Wet, Wet, Dry
2. Dry, Dry, Wet, Dry, Dry, Wet,
3. Wet, Wet, Dry, Dry, Wet, Wet, Dry, Dry

Optional: Add more options to the pattern such as Finger Touch Water (wet and dry).

Example: Touch your toe to water, touch your finger to water.

A.9 Learning Objectives

Math/Science	Language/Literacy	Problem Solving
• Finish simple patterns using two elements.	• Use words and gestures to communicate. • Follow Unfamiliar Directions.	• Identify objects by one property (i.e. wet, dry)

Notes: What did your child do well? Are there any skills they need to continue to work on?

A10. See My Way - Activity time: 15 minutes

> Materials Needed
> ☐ One (1) One Black Marker
> ☐ One (1) Blue Piece of Paper
> ☐ One (1) Orange Piece of Paper

Instructions:

Step 1: The adult should use a black marker to draw an arrow, pointing to the right, on a blue piece of paper.

Step 2: The adult should use a black marker to draw an arrow, pointing left, on an orange piece of paper.

Step 3: Tell the child they need to use their eyes to play this game.

Step 4: Move to an indoor or outdoor space where the child can take at least ten steps.

Step 5: Tell the child to take steps in the direction the arrow in pointing.

Step 6: The adult should hold up the blue piece of paper with the arrow pointing to the right. Tell child should take **two** steps to their **right.**

Step 7: Next, the adult should hold up the orange piece of paper with the arrow pointing to the left. Tell child should take **two** steps to their left.

Step 8: The adult should hold up the blue piece of paper with the arrow pointing to the right. Tell the child should take **four** steps to their right.

Step 9: The adult should hold up the orange piece of paper with the arrow pointing to the left. Tell the child should take **six** steps to their left.

Step 10: The adult should hold up the blue piece of paper with the arrow pointing to the right. Tell the child should take **eight** steps to their right.

Step 11: The adult should hold up the orange piece of paper with the arrow pointing to the left. Tell the child should take **ten** steps to their left.

Step 12: Ask the child what senses they need to use to complete this activity.
(Answer: seeing and hearing).

> **Take it to the Next Level:** Continue playing this game, picking new numbers of steps to count (Up to 20 steps).

A.10 Learning Objectives

Math/Science
- Count up to 5 objects.
- Recognize directions/symbols.

Language/Literacy
- Use words and gestures to communicate.
- Follow unfamiliar directions.

Problem Solving
- Identify colors.

Notes: What did your child do well? Are there any skills they need to continue to work on?

Behavior Tips – Supporting Age Appropriate Behavior

The purpose of Parenting Tips is to provide ideas and strategies that guide you in supporting your children to reach age appropriate social and emotional milestones. Social and Emotional Milestones include the following:

> **Social/Emotional Development**
> - Understanding safety routines.
> - Understanding personal care routines.
> - Develop self-regulation techniques.
> - Acknowledge feelings and appropriate behaviors.
> - Understand and identify feelings.
> - Understands age appropriate social interactions.
> - Communicates through words.

Order of Operation: Read through the tips and suggestions that correspond with the identified behavior. At your own pace, work through the questions in the worksheet area at the end of this section.

Part 2: Parenting Tips: Supporting Age Appropriate Behavior

> **Objective:**
>
> What are parents supposed to do when a child demonstrates anger and frustration?

Introduction:

Children's behavior can sometimes be challenging. What are parents supposed to do when a child demonstrates anger and frustration? Children's emotions can take over their body, leaving the child without the ability to reason during upsetting situations. It's important for adults to understand that the child would like to please those around them, but sometimes they need help calming their nerves or working through frustrating situations. Our five senses can be used as pathways towards calming strong emotions.

When very young children get upset, they tune out words and can become more sensitive to sounds in their environment. This may result in a more intense reaction impacted by unforeseen noises (i.e. the garbage disposal or garbage truck).

It's important to make sure that everyone in the environment is safe, including adults and children. If a child becomes overwhelmed with emotion and they start to hit the wall or bang their head, it's important to immediately redirect the behavior towards a less dangerous replacement (such as hitting a pillow). Other children and adults should keep a safe distance from the child when they're upset, as they may loose their ability to know where their body is in space, which may result in unintentionally hitting others.

If a child hits an adult while they're angry, the adult should immediately move away from the child and say, with a stern voice, "Do not hit me, that hurts." If the child approaches the adult, the adult should say, "You can talk to me when you are ready, but you are not allowed to hit me." When the child has calmed down and is ready to talk, discuss how hitting is not a way to problem solve. Tell the child, "Next time you are mad, please ask me for help."

Activity: Creating a Calming Box

Most children need support to calm down when they're upset. Using sensory related objects will help assist in transitioning a child from an "out of control" angry or overwhelmed state of being, to a calm and organized state of being, resulting in their ability to problem solve. These objects should address the five senses; touching, tasting, hearing, smelling and seeing.

A calming box can be prepared by allowing the child to place items they feel are comforting in one plastic bin. Suggested items are:

1. Touching: Something soft or squishy – a special blanket, a squishy/texture ball
2. Tasting: A cup to get a glass of water, a special flavored cracker
3. Hearing: A toy that has a parent's voice recorded on it, a card to give to a parent to request the to sing a familiar calm song.
4. Smelling: Some paper with the smell of lavender, vanilla or other calming smell on it.

5. Seeing – The ability to see a familiar adult near them so that they can seek them out for comfort.

Step 1: Tell the child you want to learn more about them and what makes them happy.
Step 2: Ask the child the following questions:

1. What's your favorite toy to touch? Why? Example: My Bear because he is soft.
2. What's your favorite food or drink to taste? Example: Carrots because they are crunchy.
3. What's your favorite song to hear? Example: Twinkle, Twinkle Little Star
4. What's your favorite smell? Example: Cookies in the Oven
5. What do you like the see when you feel hurt or sad? Example: A Band-aid

Step 3: Ask the child to help the adult fill a box with items that help them calm down. Using properties of objects listed in Step 2 (Example: Something that feels soft; food that is crunchy, etc).

It is also important for adults to have their own calming box. When a child's behavior becomes overwhelming, it's okay for parents to take a break and spend a couple of minutes with their own materials.

Some suggestions for a parent "calming" box could be:
1. Touching: Something soft or squishy – a squishy/texture ball; putting on some favorite lotion
2. Tasting: A piece of chocolate or sip of coffee
3. Hearing: A favorite song
4. Smelling: A whiff of a favorite perfume, candle or essential oil.
5. Seeing: Looking at a picture of a past vacation or a family photo

Looking for a way to help your child remember to use their calming box in an age appropriate way? Use **Soothing Sammy**, available on our website. www.jdeducational.com

Reflection

1) Have you had an experience recently with your child that you weren't sure what to say? How did you respond?

2) Next time this happens, what would be an appropriate response for your child? Keep in mind age appropriate milestones. What words does your child understand? What experiences have they had in the past that would affect the way they respond to this situation?

3) Have you seen other parents react to their children in similar situations? What did you like/dislike about the way they handled the situation?

4) Remember that you have a very hard job! It is not always easy to come up with appropriate responses in a variety of high-stress situations. Are there specific phrases or tips that you learned in this section that will make it easier for you to remember how to respond next time you are in this situation?

5) How could you use the information in this section to support family members who engage with your child when they find themselves in this situation? Would they be open to learning new tips and tricks or not?

6) What are some questions that have come up for you when filling out this section? I would love to hear your questions in our private parenting Facebook group: **JDE Parenting Tips: For Children Under 5**

Putting it into Practice

1) Write down 10 different scenarios where you may use the tips from this section:

Scenario	Your Planned Response (What will you say/do?)	Anticipated Child's Response (How will your child respond?)

2) What will you do if your child doesn't respond the way you anticipated?

Scenario	A way your child might respond (other then the anticipated response from above)	How will you respond?

Conclusion

7) Is there anything else that you would like to learn about this topic?

8) The Following Social/Emotional Learning Objectives are Designed for current Kindergarten Readiness. Circle the ones that you think your child would be able to practice in everyday situations such as those listed above.

   i. Understanding safety routines.

   ii. Understanding personal care routines.

   iii. Develop self-regulation techniques.

   iv. Acknowledge feelings and appropriate behaviors.

   v. Understand and identify feelings.

   vi. Understands age appropriate social interactions.

   vii. Communicates through words.

NOTE Section:

Thanks for playing! See you in the next Unit:
Pre-K Your Way: Level 1, Unit 5 Activities

JDEducational
Play · Learn · Grow

JDEducational
Play · Learn · Grow

Pre-K YOUR Way
Level 1 Unit 5

At the Park - Academic Activities; Creating Successful Transitions

Unit 5: Learning in the Park Academic Activities

These activities have been developed to meet specific, age-appropriate, Kindergarten-Readiness skills. These skills are specified in the learning objectives of each activity. The following activities may be completed in any order desired and are specifically designed to address the academic domains: math, science, language, literacy, cognitive, problem solving, and social-emotional development.

Each activity is on its own page. If the adult chooses to print the activities, the space below each activity is provided for adults to write notes regarding the activity. Adults are encouraged to note if the child enjoyed the activity and if the child needs to work on specific learning objectives. Each activity can be repeated more than once to enable the child to master the learning objectives designed for that activity.

A Day at the Park Activities

Individual Games

1. Blast Off
2. Stair Numbers
3. Word Kick
4. Hula Move
5. I Dig
6. Swing Me
7. Park Art

Playing with New Friends

8. New Friend Meet
9. Number Chase
10. Ready, Listen

Individual Games

A1. Blast Off - Activity time: 20 minutes

Materials Needed
- ☐ One (1) Slide
- ☐ Ten (10) 3x5 cards.
- ☐ One (1) Marker

Instructions:

Step 1: Tell your child you're going to play a **"Blast Off"** game on the slide.

Step 2: The adult should use the marker to write the numbers 1 though 10 on the 3x5 index cards (writing one number on each card).

Step 3: The adult should stand at the bottom of the slide and the child should sit at the top of the slide.

Step 4: The adult should pick one 3x5 index card and show it to the child.

Step 5: Ask the child if they can identify the number on the card.

Step 6: Starting at number 1, count to the number that is on the index card.

> **Example:** Number 7
>
> Adult and Child would count: "1,2,3,4,5,6,7" together.

Step 7: When they reach the number, the child can say **"Blast Off"** and slide down the slide.

Step 8: Repeat Steps 4 through 7 as many times as you would like.

© JDEducational: Pre-K Your Way: Level 1 Book

A.1 Learning Objectives

Math/Science
- Count up to 5 objects.
- Recognize the names of numerals.

Language/Literacy
- Participate in familiar routines.
- Understand rules and expectations related to specific places and environments.
- Use words and gestures to communicate.
- Follow simple directions.

Problem Solving
- N/A

Notes: What did your child do well? Are there any skills they need to continue to work on?

A2. Stair Numbers - Activity time: 20 minutes

Materials Needed
- ☐ A park with stairs.
- ☐ Ten (10) 3x5 cards.
- ☐ One (1) Marker

Instructions:

Step 1: Tell your child you're going to play a **"Number"** game.

Step 2: The adult should split the 3x5 index cards into two piles of 5 cards.

Step 3: The adult should use the marker to write the numbers 1 though 5 on one set of 3x5 index card piles (writing one number on each card).

Step 4: Repeat Step 3 using the other set of five 3x5 index cards.

Step 5: The adult should place one 3x5 index card from each card in Step 3 on each stair that is on the play equipment.

Step 6: The adult should hold onto the second 3x5 index card pile from Step 4.

Step 7: The adult should pick a card out of the pile that they're holding.

Step 8: Show the index card to the child and tell them to stand on the step with the same number index card on it.

> **Example:** The adult holds up a card with the number three on it.
> The child should find, and stand, on the stair that has the number three index card on it.

Step 9: The adult should repeat Steps 7 through 8, telling the child to stand on each number.

Step 10: Repeat the activity writing different numbers, letters or shapes on the sets of index cards.

A.2 Learning Objectives

Math/Science	Language/Literacy	Problem Solving
• Count up to 5 objects. • Recognize the names of numerals.	• Participate in familiar routines. • Understand rules and expectations related to specific places and environments. • Use words and gestures to communicate. • Follow simple directions.	• N/A

Notes: What did your child do well? Are there any skills they need to continue to work on?

A3. Word Kick - Activity time: 15 minutes

Materials Needed
- ☐ One (1) Large Ball to Kick
- ☐ One (1) Large Space to Kick a ball

Instructions:

Step 1: Place a large ball in an area where the child can kick the ball and not hit other children in the area.

Step 2: Tell the child this is a listening game.

Step 3: Tell the child that **before they kick the ball,** they need to **say the first letter of their name.**

Example: Name: Brandon

Child says "**B**" then kicks the ball

Step 4: Have the child continue to say the rest of the letters in their name (in order) before each kick.

Child says "**R**" then kicks the ball

Child says "**A**" then kicks the ball

Child continues until they have spelled out their name.

Take it to the Next Level: Play some more "kicking" games such as the following:

- Have the child count to a certain number (kicking the ball in between each number)
- Have the child spell names of family members.
- Have the child kick to other children at the park. Before each child kicks the ball have them say their name

A.3 Learning Objectives

Math/Science	Language/Literacy	Problem Solving
• N/A	• Participate in familiar routines. • Understand rules and expectations related to specific places and environments. • Use words and gestures to communication. • Letter identification. • Phonological Awareness. • Name Identification.	• Balance/Coordination - Kick to the correct person.

Notes: What did your child do well? Are there any skills they need to continue to work on?

A4. Hula Move - Activity time: 20 minutes

Materials Needed
- ☐ A trip to the park
- ☐ Two (2) Hula Hoops
- ☐ 3x5 number cards from Activity A1

Instructions:

Step 1: The adult should place two Hula Hoops side by side on the ground.

Step 2: The adult should put one of the 3x5 "number" index cards (Any number) in the middle of each Hula Hoop.

Step 3: Tell the child to jump inside the Hula Hoop, name the number on the index card, then jump the amount of times the number card says.

Step 4: Tell the child to jump to the other Hula Hoop and repeat Step 3.

Step 5: Repeat Steps 3 and 4 with new "number" cards.

A.4 Learning Objectives

Math/Science
- Count up to 5 objects.
- Recognize the names of numerals.

Language/Literacy
- Participate in familiar routines.
- Understand rules and expectations related to specific places and environments.
- Use words and gestures to communicate.
- Follow simple directions.

Problem Solving
- N/A

Notes: What did your child do well? Are there any skills they need to continue to work on?

A5. I Dig - Activity time: 20 minutes

Materials Needed
- ☐ Three (3) Small Green Plastic Eggs
- ☐ Three (3) Small Pink Plastic Eggs
- ☐ Three (3) Small Yellow Plastic Eggs
- ☐ One (1) Child sized sand Shovel
- ☐ One (1) Park with a sandbox
- ☐ One (1) Park that has a Sandbox

Instructions:

Step 1: The adult should hide all the plastic eggs in the sandbox.

Step 2: Tell the child to use a sand shovel to find the eggs in the sandbox. Each time they find one, have them say:

"I found an egg! It's the color __(name the color)__."

Take it to the Next Level: Are there any other materials that the adult can hide in the sandbox? These items can be categorized by size, color, shape or type.

A.5 Learning Objectives

Math/Science	Language/Literacy	Problem Solving
• N/A	• Participate in familiar routines. • Understand rules and expectations related to specific places and environments. • Use words and gestures to communicate. • Follow simple directions.	• Identify three or more colors. • Sort objects by one quality (characteristic i.e. Size, color).

Notes: What did your child do well? Are there any skills they need to continue to work on?

A6. Swing Me Activity time: 20 minutes

Materials Needed
☐ One (1) Park with Swing

Instructions:

Step 1: Tell the child you're going to push them on the swing. Each time you push them, they must say another letter in their name, until they spell their full name.

Step 2: The child should get in the swing.

Step 3: Before the adult starts to push the child in the swing, have the child say:

"**My name is_____.**"

Step 4: The child should say each letter of the child's name every time they push. See example below:

Name: Jack
Child: My name is **Jack**

Adult: Push Child in swing

Child "**J**"

Adult: Push Child in swing

Child: "**A**"

Adult: Push Child in swing

Child: "**C**"

Adult: Push Child in swing

Child: "**K**"

Adult: Push Child in swing

Take it to the Next Level: Repeat step 4 encouraging the child spell their **middle** and **last** names.

A.6 Learning Objectives

Math/Science	Language/Literacy	Problem Solving
• N/A	• Participate in familiar routines. • Understand rules and expectations related to specific places and environments. • Use words and gestures to communicate with same aged peers. • Letter Identification. • Phonological Awareness. • Name Identification. • Follow simple directions.	• N/A

Notes: What did your child do well? Are there any skills they need to continue to work on?

A7. Park Art - Activity time: 15 minutes

Materials Needed
- ☐ A park with a table
- ☐ One (1) Piece of Paper
- ☐ One (1) Box of Crayons
- ☐ One (1) Glue stick

Instructions:

Step 1: Have the child sit at a table with the crayons and paper for an art break.

Step 2: Tell the child to use the crayons to draw a picture of the park you're at.

Step 3: Ask your child to collect items they see on the ground that they want to glue on their picture.

> **Example:**
> - Fallen leaves
> - Sticks
> - Broken flower petals

Step 4: The adult should help the child glue the items from Step 3 on their picture.

Step 5: Ask the child about the picture they drew of the park. Ask them what their favorite part is.

A.7 Learning Objectives

Math/Science	Language/Literacy	Problem Solving
• Exploring Nature	• Participate in familiar routines. • Understand rules and expectations related to specific places and environments. • Use words and gestures to communicate. • Answering open-ended questions. • Following simple directions.	• Visual Representation (Art)

Notes: What did your child do well? Are there any skills they need to continue to work on?

Park Games with Others

A8. New Friend Meet - Activity time: 20 minutes

Materials Needed
- ☐ A safe neighborhood park with other children

Instructions:

Step 1: Have the children stand in an area together.

Step 2: Tell the children they're going to learn each other's names. The adult is going to give a child an action to complete before each child says their name.

Step 3: Start with one child by giving them the following direction:

- **Clap, Clap**, Say your name

Step 4: Allow each child to repeat step 3 until all of the children have had a turn.

Step 5: Repeat Step 3 with the following directions:

- **Spin, Spin**, Say your name
- **Jump, Jump,** Say your name
- **Sit Down, Stand Up**, Say your name
- **Tap your head, Tap your Toes**, Say your name
- **Hop on one foot, Hop on the other foot**, Say your name
- **Shake your arms, Shake your feet**, Say your name

Step 6: Allow the children to take turns coming up with an action for the children to do before saying their names.

Take it to the next level: Have the child repeat a movement pattern before saying their names. Can they finish the pattern on their own?

Example: Clap, Jump, Jump, Clap, Jump, Jump, Say your name.

A.8 Learning Objectives

Math/Science	Language/Literacy	Problem Solving
• N/A	• Participate in familiar routines. • Understand rules and expectations related to specific places and environments. • Use words and gestures to communicate with same aged peers. • Demonstrate awareness of the meaning of the behaviors of others. • Use words to problem solve and respond to a variety of social situations. • Name recognition. • Following new directions.	• Introduction to patterns.

Notes: What did your child do well? Are there any skills they need to continue to work on?

A9. Number Chase - Activity time: 15 minutes

Materials Needed
- ☐ A safe neighborhood park with other children

Instructions:

Step 1: Tell the children they're going to play a **chase game.**

Step 2: Follow these directions:
- When the adult says the **number 3,** that means to **run fast.**
- When the adult says the **number 2,** they should **walk slow.**
- When the adult says the **number 1**, they should **freeze/stop** where they are.

Step 3: To start the game, the adult should say "number 3" and all the children should start running.

Step 4: Continue saying different numbers, having the children follow the directions in Step 2 when they hear each number.

Take it to the Next Level: Allow the children to take turns picking the numbers.

1 2 3

© JDEducational: Pre-K Your Way: Level 1 Book

A.9 Learning Objectives

Math/Science
- Count up to 5 objects.
- Recognize the names of numerals.

Language/Literacy
- Participate in familiar routines.
- Understand rules and expectations related to specific places and environments.
- Use words and gestures to communicate with same aged peers.
- Demonstrate awareness of the meaning of the behaviors of others.
- Use words to problem solve and respond to a variety of social situations.

Problem Solving
- Introduction to Symbolic meaning

Notes: What did your child do well? Are there any skills they need to continue to work on?

A10. Ready, Listen - Activity time: 15 minutes

Materials Needed
- ☐ A safe neighborhood park with other children
- ☐ Two (2) Orange Cones or Ball (any color)

Instructions:

Step 1: Tell the children they're going to play a **running game**.

Step 2: The adult should place the cones (or the balls) **12 feet apart** from each other.

Step 3: Have the children line up next to one of the cones/balls.

Step 4: The adult should first say:

All children wearing blue, run!

Step 5: The children wearing the color blue should run to the other ball/cone.

Step 6: The adult should continue naming colors of clothing items that the children are wearing until all children have run to the second cone/ball.

Take it to the Next Level: Use the following adjectives to direct which children should run:

1. What **type of shoes** they're wearing (sandals, tennis shoes)
2. What **color eyes** they have.
3. What **letter their name starts with**.
4. Anything else that you can think of.

A.10 Learning Objectives

Math/Science	Language/Literacy	Problem Solving
• N/A	• Participate in familiar routines. • Understand rules and expectations related to specific places and environments. • Use words and gestures to communicate with same aged peers. • Demonstrate awareness of the meaning of the behaviors of others. • Use words to problem solve and respond to a variety of social situations. • Follow new directions.	• Identify three or more colors.

Notes: What did your child do well? Are there any skills they need to continue to work on?

Tips – Creating Successful Transitions

The purpose of Parenting Tips is to provide ideas and strategies that guide you in supporting your children to reach age appropriate social and emotional milestones. Social and Emotional Milestones include the following:

> **Social/Emotional Development**
> - Understanding safety routines.
> - Understanding personal care routines.
> - Develop self-regulation techniques.
> - Acknowledge feelings and appropriate behaviors.
> - Understand and identify feelings.
> - Understands age appropriate social interactions.
> - Communicates through words.

Order of Operation: Read through the tips and suggestions that correspond with the identified behavior. At your own pace, work through the questions in the worksheet area at the end of this section.

> **Objective:**
>
> How do I teach my child easily transition from one activity to another?

Introduction:

Transitioning from one activity to another, or from one place to another can be challenging with children. Sometimes children don't want to leave the current location, resulting in a power struggle between parents and their children. When interrupted with a request to leave immediately, children are expected to stop in the midst of their idea/plan. Transition warnings allow children to anticipate a transition before it's requested, finish their current play and have enough time to process the request of separating from a specific location. Transition warnings should be given verbally and visually, multiple times, prior to the transition occurring. Some children also benefit from a physical prompt, such as looking them in the eye, placing a hand onto their shoulder or their back to gain attention.

Appropriate transition warnings include:
1) Five minutes before it is time to leave, the adult should look the child in the eye and tell them that they will be leaving in five minutes.
2) Two minutes before it is time to leave, the adult should look the child in the eye and tell them that they will be leaving in two minutes. Make sure to tell the child where you are going.
3) When it is time to leave, the adult should look the child in the eye and tell the child it is time to go and where they are going.
4) Hold the child's hand and walk to the car.

After giving appropriate transition warnings, tell the child that you understand they enjoy being at the current location, and they will be able to return one day. As you're leaving, explain to the child where they're going and what you're going to do there.

Consistency is key. Make sure to give transition warnings every time you leave a location. In time, the child will understand what the time frames refer to and will learn that when the adult approaches them the third time, it will be time to leave.

Visual and Auditory cues:

For younger children, a visual and auditory cue may help with transitions. Here are some ways to incorporate visual and auditory cues in transition warnings:

1. Use a timer on a cell phone to cue each warning (Set the timer for 5 minutes so the child knows that when they hear the timer, it's time to go).
2. When the adult gives the child a transition warning, help the child count their fingers to see how many minutes until it is time to leave (For Example: If it's a two minute warning, help your child point to two of their fingers).
3. Transitional objects can create visual and tactile supports when a child needs to move to a new location. The objects may include a special stuffed animal, or cup of water/snack they can hold when they're leaving one place and going to another.

If a child doesn't want to leave a location, and starts to tantrum, the adult should sit next to the child and let them cry. When the child has calmed down, the adult should repeat that it's time to leave, and offer them a transition object. Repeat this process until the child is ready to leave.

If your child tends to become upset when it is time to leave a specific place, the adult should add another warning step by adding an extra transition warning ahead to the sequence. For example - start the warnings at 10 minutes before it's time to leave (instead of 5 minutes). This will allow the child to have more time to prepare for the upcoming transition, resulting with more of a willingness to leave when told.

Consistency is key. The adult should not "negotiate" with the child when it is time to leave. If the child requests to stay at the location longer and the adult agrees, the child will continue to "negotiate" the leaving time in future situations. The adult should follow through with leaving the place when requested by the adult, reinforcing that when the adult says it is time to leave, then it truly is time to leave.

Leaving a place can be hard for children, especially if they are still in the middle of completing a task. Transition warnings, combined with consistency from adults, will teach children to become compliant when asked to leave a place.

Reflection

1) Have you had an experience recently with your child that you weren't sure what to say? How did you respond?

2) Next time this happens, what would be an appropriate response for your child? Keep in mind age appropriate milestones. What words does your child understand? What experiences have they had in the past that would affect the way they respond to this situation?

3) Have you seen other parents react to their children in similar situations? What did you like/dislike about the way they handled the situation?

4) Remember that you have a very hard job! It is not always easy to come up with appropriate responses in a variety of high-stress situations. Are there specific phrases or tips that you learned in this section that will make it easier for you to remember how to respond next time you are in this situation?

5) How could you use the information in this section to support family members who engage with your child when they find themselves in this situation? Would they be open to learning new tips and tricks or not?

6) What are some questions that have come up for you when filling out this section? I would love to hear your questions in our private parenting Facebook group: **JDE Parenting Tips: For Children Under 5**

Putting it into Practice

1) Write down 10 different scenarios where you may use the tips from this section:

Scenario	Your Planned Response (What will you say/do?)	Anticipated Child's Response (How will your child respond?)

2) What will you do if your child doesn't respond the way you anticipated?

Scenario	A way your child might respond (other then the anticipated response from above)	How will you respond?

Conclusion

9) Is there anything else that you would like to learn about this topic?

10) The Following Social/Emotional Learning Objectives are Designed for current Kindergarten Readiness. Circle the ones that you think your child would be able to practice in everyday situations such as those listed above.

   i. Understanding safety routines.

   ii. Understanding personal care routines.

   iii. Develop self-regulation techniques.

   iv. Acknowledge feelings and appropriate behaviors.

   v. Understand and identify feelings.

   vi. Understands age appropriate social interactions.

   vii. Communicates through words.

NOTE Section:

....
Thanks for playing! See you in the next Unit:
Pre-K Your Way: Level 1, Unit 6 Activities

JDEducational
Play · Learn · Grow

JDEducational
Play · Learn · Grow

Pre-K YOUR Way
Level 1 Unit 6

Investigating Nutrition; Trying New Foods

Unit 6: Investigating Nutrition Themed Academic Activities

These activities have been developed to meet specific, age-appropriate, Kindergarten-Readiness skills. These skills are specified in the learning objectives of each activity. The following activities may be completed in any order desired and are specifically designed to address the academic domains: math, science, language, literacy, cognitive, problem solving, and social-emotional development.

Each activity is on its own page. If the adult chooses to print the activities, the space below each activity is provided for adults to write notes regarding the activity. Adults are encouraged to note if the child enjoyed the activity and if the child needs to work on specific learning objectives. Each activity can be repeated more than once to enable the child to master the learning objectives designed for that activity.

Investigating Nutrition Activities

1. Food Groups
2. Ready, Eat!
3. Colors of My Fruit
4. My Favorite Meal
5. Food that Grows
6. The Ity Bity Seed
7. Egg, Scramble, Roll
8. Food Mix
9. Menu Mix
10. Recipe Delight

> **Take it to the Next Level:**
>
> There are some activities which have a component included on how to take an activity to "the next level", increasing skill level related to the learning objectives laid out in that specific activity. Once the child has successful completed an activity, adults are encouraged to try the "take it to the next level."

© JDEducational: Pre-K Your Way: Level 1 Book

A1. Food Groups - Activity time: 20 minutes

Materials Needed
- ☐ Grocery Store Sale Paper
- ☐ Child-safe Scissors
- ☐ Six (6) Paper Plates
- ☐ One (1) Glue Stick

Instructions:

Step 1: The adult should use a pen to write the following words on each paper plate (write one word per plate):

- Fruit
- Vegetable
- Meat
- Dairy
- Bread
- Sweets

Step 2: Tell the child to **match pictures** from the **sale paper ads**, to the **correct plate**.

Step 3: Help the child use child-safe scissors to cut out pictures of different foods from the sale paper ads. (Make sure there are at least two food pictures per category stated in Step 1.)

Step 4: Ask the child to **organize the foods by category**, placing each cut-out food picture onto the correct plate.

Step 5: Allow the child to use a glue stick to glue the foods onto each plate.

Take it to the Next Level: Keep the plates out for the rest of the week and allow the child to keep track of foods they eat during meals. Are there food categories they eat more of or less of?

A.1 Learning Objectives

Math/Science	Language/Literacy	Problem Solving
• N/A	• Participate in familiar routines. • Understand rules and expectations related to specific places and environments. • Use words and gestures to communicate. • Follow new directions	• Sort objects by one quality (characteristic i.e. Size, color) • Understand Different vs. Same.

Notes: What did your child do well? Are there any skills they need to continue to work on?

A2. Ready, Eat! - Activity time: 20 minutes

Materials Needed
- ☐ One (1) Fruit the child could eat
- ☐ One (1) Plate
- ☐ One (1) Sink
- ☐ One (1) Clean Kitchen Towel
- ☐ One (1) Knife for the adult to use

Instructions:

Step 1: Tell the child that when it's time to make a meal, there is a food preparation process to follow.

Step 2: When someone wants to eat a piece of fruit, they must wash it, dry it and sometimes cut it (sometimes cook it) before it's ready to eat.

Step 3: Tell the child they're going to practice preparing their food.

Step 4: The adult should ask the child to hold the piece of fruit.

Step 5: Ask the child to wash the fruit in a bucket of clean water or in the sink.

Step 6: Tell the child to dry the fruit with the clean dishtowel.

Step 7: Allow the child to watch the adult cut the fruit into child-safe pieces.

Step 8: Now, tell the child it's time to eat!

Take it to the Next Level: Allow the child to prepare another fruit with an adult's help. Is there a vegetable they can prepare for the adult to cook?

A.2 Learning Objectives

Math/Science	Language/Literacy	Problem Solving
• Introduction to Process/Meal Preperation	• Participate in familiar routines. • Understand rules and expectations related to specific places and environments. • Use words and gestures to communicate. • Follow simple directions.	• N/A

Notes: What did your child do well? Are there any skills they need to continue to work on?

A3. Colors of My Fruit - Activity time: 15 minutes

Materials Needed
- ☐ One (1) Box of Crayons
- ☐ A variety of fruits and vegetables
- ☐ One (1) Piece of paper

Instructions:

Step 1: The adult should put a variety of fruits and vegetables on a table for the child to see.

Step 2: Tell the child to take the crayons out of the box and place them on the table.

Step 3: Tell the child to pick one crayon.

Step 4: Tell the child to find all of the fruits and veggies on the table that match the same crayon color they chose is Step 3.

Step 5: Ask the child to count the total amount of fruits and vegetables from Step 4.

Step 6: Tell the child to use the crayon from step 3 to draw the same amount of tallies they counted in Step 5.

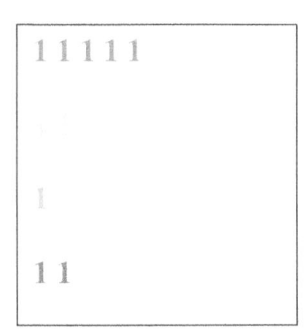

```
1 1 1 1 1


1

1 1
```

Step 7: Repeat Steps 2 through 6 until the child has gone through all of the crayon colors. If there are no fruits or veggies that match their crayon color, then tell them they will not draw any tally marks.

Step 8: When completed, ask the child to count each set of tally marks. Ask them which colors matched most of the foods? Which colors didn't match any foods?

A.3 Learning Objectives

Math/Science
- One to one correspondence.
- Understanding numbers.
- Quantity and Counting

Language/Literacy
- Participate in familiar routines.
- Understand rules and expectations related to specific places and environments.
- Use words and gestures to communicate.
- Follow simple directions.
- Building vocabulary.

Problem Solving
- Identify three or more colors.
- Sort objects by one quality (characteristic i.e. Size, color)

Notes: What did your child do well? Are there any skills they need to continue to work on?

A4. My Favorite Meal - Activity time: 20 minutes

> **Materials Needed**
> ☐ One (1) Box of Crayons
> ☐ One (1) Pen
> ☐ Two (2) Pieces of Paper

Instructions:

Step 1: Tell the child they're going to create a story about their favorite meal.

Step 2: The adult should write down the following story on one sheet of paper and have the child fill in the blanks with their answer:

"When I make my favorite meal, I eat it all up. It's good for my stomach to get healthy food so my body can grow. For breakfast, I like to eat _____. I eat my breakfast first. For lunch I like to eat _____. I eat my lunch after my breakfast. For dinner I like to eat _____. I eat my dinner at the end of my day. Sometimes I eat snacks. My favorite snacks are _____."

Step 3: Allow the child to use the crayons to draw pictures of the foods they named on the blank piece of paper.

A.4 Learning Objectives

Math/Science	Language/Literacy	Problem Solving
• Understanding the impact of food on your body.	• Participate in familiar routines. • Understand rules and expectations related to specific places and environments. • Use words and gestures to communicate. • Answer open-ended questions. • Follow simple directions.	• Introduction to visual symbols.

Notes: What did your child do well? Are there any skills they need to continue to work on?

A5. Food that Grows - Activity time: 20 minutes

Materials Needed
- ☐ An area that is safe for the child to jump.

Instructions:

Step 1: Tell the child that a lot of foods grow from seeds. When a seed is planted, some foods grow up above the ground, and some foods grow down, below the ground.

Step 2: Tell the child you're going to play a listening game. The adult is going to name a type of food and then say "up" or "down".

- When the adult says **"up"**, the child should jump up. That means that **food grows above the ground.**
- When the adult says **"down"**, the child should sit down. This means that **food grows below the ground.**

Step 3: The adult should say the following foods and action words:

- Green Beans grow **UP** (child should Jump)
- Onions grow **DOWN** (child should sit down).
- Potatoes grow **DOWN** (child should stay sitting).
- Peas grow **UP** (child should jump up).
- Zucchini grow **UP** (child should jump).
- Carrots grow **DOWN** (child should sit down).
- Strawberries grow **UP** (child should jump up).
- Radishes grown **DOWN** (child should sit down).

Take it to the Next Level: Continue Step 3 with more foods that grow up or down.

Say the description words in a pattern form. **Example:**

1. Onions grow Down
2. Potatoes grow Down
3. Peas grow Up

4. Carrots grow Down
5. Radishes grow Down
6. Strawberries grow Up

A.5 Learning Objectives

Math/Science
- Introduction to opposites.
- Finish simple patterns using two elements.

Language/Literacy
- Participate in familiar routines.
- Understand rules and expectations related to specific places and environments.
- Use words and gestures to communicate.
- Follow simple directions.

Problem Solving
- Sort objects by one quality (characteristic i.e. Size, color)
- Understand Different vs. Same.

Notes: What did your child do well? Are there any skills they need to continue to work on?

A6. The Itty Bitty Seed - Activity time: 20 minutes

Materials Needed
- ☐ One (1) Packet of Pumpkin Seeds
- ☐ One (1) Packet of Butternut Squash Seeds
- ☐ One (1) Packet of Carrot Seeds
- ☐ One (1) Packet of Pea Seeds
- ☐ One (1) Packet of Romaine Lettuce Seeds
- ☐ One (1) Packet of Green Beans Seeds
- ☐ One (1) Packet of Radish Seeds
- ☐ One (1) Packet of Tomato Seeds
- ☐ One (1) Packet of Strawberry Seeds
- ☐ Three (3) Buckets
- ☐ One (1) Green Crayon
- ☐ One (1) Orange Crayon
- ☐ One (1) Red Crayon

Instructions:

Step 1: Tell the child that seeds grow into different foods. They need to be planted in dirt, drink water and be warmed by the sun.

Step 2: The adult should place the three empty buckets on the table.

Step 3: The adult should put a red crayon in one bucket, a green crayon in another bucket and an orange crayon in the last bucket.

Step 4: Put the packets of seeds on the table in front of the child. Tell the child that some of these foods are orange, some are red and some are green.

Step 5: Tell the child to put the foods that will grow green in the bucket with the green crayon, orange in the bucket with the orange crayon and red in the bucket with the red crayon.

Step 6: Have the child repeat the following phrases filling in the names of the seeds:

"The _____, _____ and _____ will grow to be green"

Step 7: Continue with the rest of the colors.

© JDEducational: Pre-K Your Way: Level 1 Book

A.6 Learning Objectives

Math/Science	Language/Literacy	Problem Solving
• N/A	• Participate in familiar routines. • Understand rules and expectations related to specific places and environments. • Use words and gestures to communicate. • Follow new directions.	• Identify three or more colors. • Sort objects by one quality (characteristic i.e. Size, color) • Understand Different vs. Same.

Notes: What did your child do well? Are there any skills they need to continue to work on?

A7. Egg, Scramble, Roll - Activity time: 15 minutes

Materials Needed
- ☐ A large area where the child can move around safely and roll on the floor.

Instructions:

Step 1: Tell the child they're going to pretend they're an egg. When people want to cook an egg, some like to eat it scrambled. They're going to pretend to become a scrambled egg.

Step 2: Tell the child they're going to do an egg dance.

Directions for egg dance:

- When the adult says, "**crack the egg**", the child should drop to the **ground.**
- When the adult says, "**scramble the egg**" the child should **spin in a circle**.
- When the adult says, "**cook the egg**", the child should **lie on the floor and roll.**

Step 3: The adult should say the following patterns and encourage the child to respond by completing the movements from Step 2.

- Scramble, Scramble, Cook, Cook (Repeat pattern three times)
- Crack, Crack, Scramble, Cook (Repeat pattern three times)
- Scramble, Cook, Scramble, Cook (Repeat pattern three times)
- Crack, Scramble, Scramble, Cook (Repeat pattern three times)

Take it to the Next Level: Can the adult or child think of some more patterns using the above words and actions?

A.7 Learning Objectives

Math/Science
- Finish simple patterns using two elements.

Language/Literacy
- Participate in familiar routines.
- Understand rules and expectations related to specific places and environments.
- Follow new directions.

Problem Solving
- Gross Motor: Motor Planning
- Follow auditory cues.

Notes: What did your child do well? Are there any skills they need to continue to work on?

A8. Food Mix - Activity time: 15 minutes

Materials Needed
- ☐ An open place where the child can move.

Instructions:

Step 1: Tell the child the adult is going to name different food items. **Each item is going to have its own dance step.**

Step 2: The dance steps are:

- Apple and Bananas and Grapes – **Clap, Clap, Clap – Those are Fruits**
- Zucchini and Tomatoes and Broccoli- **Jump, Jump, Jump – Those are Vegetables**
- Milk and Yogurt and Cheese – **Spin, Spin, Spin – those are Dairy Products**
- Cake and Ice Cream and Candy Bars – **Stomp, Stomp, Stomp – Those are Sweets.**

Step 3: Create a Pattern with the Foods from above. Give the child two-step directions when telling them to move. For example:

- Apple – **Clap**; Zucchini – **Jump**; Apple – **Clap**; Zucchini - **Jump**
- Milk – **Spin**; Ice Cream- **Stomp**; Milk – **Spin**; Ice Cream- **Stomp**

Take it to the Next Level: Continue grouping food items together that the child eats. Create three step patterns. For Example:

- Apple – Clap; Zucchini – Jump; Milk – Spin; Apple – Clap; Zucchini – Jump; Milk – Spin.

© JDEducational: Pre-K Your Way: Level 1 Book

A.8 Learning Objectives

Math/Science

- Finish simple patterns using two elements.

Language/Literacy

- Participate in familiar routines.
- Understand rules and expectations related to specific places and environments.
- Use words and gestures to communicate with same aged peers.
- Follow new directions.

Problem Solving

- Sort objects by one quality (characteristic i.e. Size, color)
- Understand Different vs. Same.
- Follow auditory cues.

Notes: What did your child do well? Are there any skills they need to continue to work on?

A9. Menu Mix - Activity time: 15 minutes

Materials Needed
- ☐ One (1) Box of Crayons
- ☐ One (1) Grocery Sale Paper Ads
- ☐ One (1) Child sized scissors
- ☐ Four (4) Pieces of Blank Paper
- ☐ One (1) Glue Stick

Instructions:

Step 1: Tell the child to pick **four different color crayons** out of a box of crayons.

Step 2: Tell the child to put one crayon on each piece of paper.

Step 3: Tell the child to look for items in the sale paper that match the color crayons they picked out.

Step 5: Allow the child to use child-sized scissors to cut out the items they find.

Step 6: Encourage the child to use a glue stick to glue the items onto the piece of paper that has the same color crayon on it.

Take it to the Next Level: Repeat Step 1 through Step 6 with four new colors.

A.9 Learning Objectives

Math/Science
- N/A

Language/Literacy
- Participate in familiar routines.
- Understand rules and expectations related to specific places and environments.
- Use words and gestures to communicate.
- Follow new directions.

Problem Solving
- Identify three or more colors.
- Sort objects by one quality (characteristic i.e. Size, color)
- Understand Different vs. Same.

Notes: What did your child do well? Are there any skills they need to continue to work on?

A10. Recipe Delight - Activity time: 15 minutes

Materials Needed
- ☐ One (1) Jar of Peanut Butter
  - ○ **CAUTION** - If the child is allergic to PB or unable to eat a PB and Jelly sandwich, see the "Take it to the Next Level" section in the Instructions below.
- ☐ One (1) Jar of Jelly
- ☐ One (1) Loaf of Bread
- ☐ One (1) Jar/Cup of Applesauce
- ☐ One (1) Bag of Baby Carrots
- ☐ One (1) Gallon of Milk
- ☐ One (1) Roll of Painter's Tape

Instructions:

Step 1: Tell the child that this activity describes **how to follow a recipe**.

Step 2: The adult should find an indoor or outdoor area where painter's tape can be placed on the floor.

Step 3: The adult should use painter's tap to place **two, three-foot long lines,** on the **floor, three feet apart from each other.**

Step 3: The adult should place all the food items in a row on one line.

Step 4: Tell the child they're going to find items they need to make a peanut butter and jelly sandwich.

Step 5: Tell the child to find the loaf of bread.

Step 6: When they find it, have them pick up the loaf of bread and move it to the taped line that has no food on it.

Step 7: Next, tell the child they need the peanut butter. Have them find the jar of peanut butter and put it on the right side of the loaf of bread.

© JDEducational: Pre-K Your Way: Level 1 Book

Step 8: Next, tell the child that they need jelly. Have them find the jar of jelly and put in next to the jar of peanut butter.

Step 9: Ask the child to look at the rest of the items on the line. Do they use any of those items when making a peanut butter and jelly sandwich? (**Answer: No**).

Step 10: Yay! They found all of the items that they would need for the Peanut Butter and Jelly Sandwich recipe.

Take it to the Next Level:

Repeat Step 3 through Step 10 using a family recipe that you usually make. Make sure to display some extra items so the child understands that different foods are used for different recipes.

Some examples could include:
- Homemade Macaroni and Cheese
- Pancakes
- Chocolate Chip Cookies
- Banana Bread

A.10 Learning Objectives

Math/Science	Language/Literacy	Problem Solving
• Understanding that parts make a whole.	• Participate in familiar routines. • Understand rules and expectations related to specific places and environments. • Use words and gestures to communicate. • Follow new directions.	• Sort objects by one quality (characteristic i.e. Size, color)

Notes: What did your child do well? Are there any skills they need to continue to work on?

Tips – Introducing Children to New Foods

The purpose of Parenting Tips is to provide ideas and strategies that guide you in supporting your children to reach age appropriate social and emotional milestones. Social and Emotional Milestones include the following:

> **Social/Emotional Development**
> - Understanding safety routines.
> - Understanding personal care routines.
> - Develop self-regulation techniques.
> - Acknowledge feelings and appropriate behaviors.
> - Understand and identify feelings.
> - Understands age appropriate social interactions.
> - Communicates through words.

Order of Operation: Read through the tips and suggestions that correspond with the identified behavior. At your own pace, work through the questions in the worksheet area at the end of this section.

> **Objective:**
>
> How do I introduce new foods to my child?

Parenting Tips:

Mealtime can be challenging for families with young children, especially families with children that are "picky" eaters. The trick to surviving mealtime is to have consistent mealtime expectations, while also providing an environment that makes mealtime fun. If mealtime feels like a chore or is filled with negative experiences, children will learn to do their best to avoid mealtime. When introducing foods to young children, it is important that another adult is eating with the child. This allows the child to see another person eat a variety of foods and enjoys them.

If you have a child that refuses to try certain foods, make sure the child doesn't have any food allergies. Sometimes children feel funny after eating certain foods that can trigger a type of food sensitivity or food allergy. Food sensitivities can produce a variety of symptoms that may include a significant allergic reaction, an upset stomach, constipation or gas. It's always important to speak to the child's pediatrician if they're avoiding certain foods on a regular basis. Check the following website for foods that can trigger common childhood allergies:
The American College of Allergy, Asthma and Immunology: http://acaai.org/allergies/types/food-allergy

When introducing new foods to young children, make sure the child is able to bite, chew and swallow successfully. Before introducing a new food to the child, ask yourself: Is the food too chewy? Too hard to bite? Too spicy? These are all important characteristics of foods to consider before introducing it to a child. It may take multiple exposures of the same food before a child will put it in their mouth, or try it for a second time. After trying a new food, it may take up to twenty more introductions, of the same food, before the child feels comfortable adding it to their usual repertoire.

Eating should be a pleasurable experience. It's important to remember that adults have food preferences also. Allowing a child to have input on foods they place in their body helps them to process their feelings about the food, in turn creating a positive connection with a food item. Some foods have different textures: slimy, crunchy, cold, hot, spicy, etc. When a child touches food with their hands, they're investigating that food, learning about texture and smell before they place it in their mouth. Eating uses all of the senses (taste, touch, sight, smell and sometimes sound (crunchy). Allowing children time to investigate new foods will help children understand the properties of each food item and determine what they expect when they place it in their mouth.

Choices are key when creating a positive eating environment. If a family is having two vegetables, pasta, a salad and meat for dinner, allow the child to pick which vegetable they would like to have on their plate. Choices allow children to feel as though they were able to have some type of input into what they will be placing in their body. It's not recommended to let a child choose a food item that the rest of the family is not eating.

Suggestions for Mealtime Rules:

1. The child will sit at the table with the rest of the family, engaging in conversation with no technology/screen time.
2. Feed the child the same foods the rest of the family is eating.
3. Allow the child to use their hands and other senses to investigate new foods.
4. While eating, the child must stay seated in their highchair/chair.
5. All food must stay at the table.

Suggestions for Introducing New Foods:

1. Allow the child to use a spoon to scoop how much of the new food they want on their plate.
2. Allow the child to touch the food and place it in their mouth at their own pace.
3. Don't force the child to eat the new food. Once they taste it, ask them what they think about it and offer more.
4. If the child says no thank you, leave the food on their plate and allow them to revisit it later.
5. Re-introduce the same food two or three more times during the same week.

Children like to have control of new situations, including mealtime. Here are some ways to allow a child to control their food:

1. Allow the child to pick where the food on their plate should be placed.
2. Allow the child to decide how many scoops of certain foods are placed on their plate.
3. Allow the child to pick the type and color of plates/cups/silverware.
4. Allow the child to take breaks throughout their meal.

Consistency is key. Make sure that mealtime rules are followed at every meal. Children thrive on routine and consistency. Allowing the child to have one spot they sit at during each meal allows the child to build visual boundaries regarding movement during mealtime.

Parent Reflection

1) Have you had an experience recently with your child that you weren't sure what to say? How did you respond?

2) Next time this happens, what would be an appropriate response for your child? Keep in mind age appropriate milestones. What words does your child understand? What experiences have they had in the past that would affect the way they respond to this situation?

3) Have you seen other parents react to their children in similar situations? What did you like/dislike about the way they handled the situation?

4) Remember that you have a very hard job! It is not always easy to come up with appropriate responses in a variety of high-stress situations. Are there specific phrases or tips that you learned in this section that will make it easier for you to remember how to respond next time you are in this situation?

5) How could you use the information in this section to support family members who engage with your child when they find themselves in this situation? Would they be open to learning new tips and tricks or not?

6) What are some questions that have come up for you when filling out this section? I would love to hear your questions in our private parenting Facebook group: JDE Parenting Tips: For Children Under 5

Putting it into Practice

1) Write down 10 different scenarios where you may use the tips from this section:

Scenario	Your Planned Response (What will you say/do?)	Anticipated Child's Response (How will your child respond?)

2) What will you do if your child doesn't respond the way you anticipated?

Scenario	A way your child might respond (other then the anticipated response from above)	How will you respond?

Conclusion

1) Is there anything else that you would like to learn about this topic?

2) The Following Social/Emotional Learning Objectives are Designed for current Kindergarten Readiness. Circle the ones that you think your child would be able to practice in everyday situations such as those listed above.

   i. Understanding safety routines.

   ii. Understanding personal care routines.

   iii. Develop self-regulation techniques.

   iv. Acknowledge feelings and appropriate behaviors.

   v. Understand and identify feelings.

   vi. Understands age appropriate social interactions.

   vii. Communicates through words.

NOTE Section:

Thanks for playing! See you in the next Unit:
Pre-K Your Way: Level 1, Unit 12 Activities

JDEducational
Play · Learn · Grow

Looking for More support with Social Skill Development?

Introducing: Soothing Sammy Social Skills Set (by JDEducational):

1. **The "Soothing Sammy" children's story** teaches children how to calm down when they are upset. In the book, children visit Sammy, at his dog house. Sammy teaches them how to calm down, identify why they were mad and encourage them to create a solution. Your child will learn:

- How to process emotions.
- How to communicate feelings.
- How to problem-solve.
- How to use their sensory system to calm down.

2. **Sammy the Plush dog** - Learn how to **construct a "Sammy house" for Sammy, the plush toy dog (included) to live in.** Sammy's house incorporates common household items talked about in the "Soothing Sammy" book. These items help children calm down when they are upset. This house **helps children and families implement the calming strategies learned in the Sammy book.**

- Sammy meets and exceeds all US safety Standards for children ages 2 years old and up.
- Machine Washable
- 10 inches long

3. **The activity guide discusses a variety of ways which your family can incorporate Sammy's lessons into your everyday life,** including:

- Sharing space and items with other children.
- Encouraging your child to listen.
- Helping your child express their feelings.
- Preventing your child from becoming frustrated.
- Transitioning to and from different activities.
- Following Directions.

This Sammy set teaches children how to manage their emotions in a way they will understand, remember and implement. The children's book, along with Sammy the plush dog and parent guide, creates a complementary set of tools that supports your child's emotional development. Sammy's techniques give children the confidence to manage their emotions.

Customer Reviews

⭐⭐⭐⭐⭐

5   Everyone needs this set!

Parenting is hard work! Children do not come with instructions, so knowing how to handle their emotional needs is so hard. Thanks to Soothing Sammy I am better equipped to help my children through their melt-downs and tantrums. Since grabbing this set I have seen not only a difference in my children but a difference in how I handle them in the hard moments. I definitely recommend this set to every parent.

- Stephanie E on Mar 08, 2018

5   **Soothing Sammy -**

My daughter and I had fun reading and building Sammy's house. She loves Sammy! So far it has helped her feel better when upset. She has chosen something to crunch on when mad and then hugging Sammy when sad. We keep it in the living room where she will hopefully continue to use it.

- Jennifer S. on Feb 26, 2018

5   Just What We Needed-

Like many kids, my 3-year-old often gets sad and has a hard time expressing himself. Soothing Sammy has helped him identify a toolkit full of tools that he can choose from based on the situation. The tools allow him to calm down, sooth, and verbally express himself so we can address the reasoning behind his emotion.

-Nancy on Feb 11, 2018

5   Excited for Sammy

I order Sammy for my 7-year-old son who sometimes gets angry and has a hard time controlling his emotions. Sammy arrived today and he was very excited to see what he was about. We read the book together and have already talk about how he was going to decorate his home. I am hopeful that this is going to be a great teaching tool for him and that Sammy is going to become a big part of helping him control his emotions. We are very excited to but these new teaching tools into our everyday lives. Sammy is super cute and the book is at a reading level that young children can read on their own.

- *Heidi on Feb 03, 2018*

More Pre-K Your Way Activities:

Level 1: Social Emotional Skill Curriculum

**Note: *This level is appropriate for children of all ages, regardless of academic level.*

* Themed Academic Activities which use items found around the home to teach math, science, language, literacy, pre-writing skills to meet **Level 1 Learning Objectives**. Skills are taught through daily activities such as going to the park, all about me, all about my family, nutrition and MORE!

* Behavior Support Tips & Worksheets - Parenting Tip sections that provide ideas and strategies for parents which support age-appropriate social and emotional milestones. These tips include helping their child Understand Diversity, Take Turns with Loved Ones and MORE!

Level 2: Intermediate Academic Curriculum (Alphabet and More)

* Themed Academic Activities which use items found around the home to teach math, science, language, literacy, pre-writing skills to meet **Level 2 Learning Objectives!**

Themes include: My Community, Roadways and Signs, Advanced Opposites, Space Exploration and MORE!

The Playful Alphabet: Activities teach letter identification and writing skills through art, sensory activities, reading, movement activities (dancing, jumping, running) and language arts. Five (5) Activities for each letter plus alphabet review games.

Level 3: Advanced Academic Curriculum

* Themed Academic Activities which use items found around the home to teach math, science, language, literacy, pre-writing skills to meet **Level 3 Learning Objectives!**

Themes include: Camping, Transportation, Planet Earth, Construction, Oceanography and MORE!

Projects: include all academic and social learning objectives. Each project guides the child to develop a hypothesis, research answers and form a conclusion.
Projects include: Transportation: Understanding Package Delivery Systems, Project Weather: Discovering the Elements, Project Earth: Reduce, Reuse and Recycle, Project Construction: Building Components and Design and MORE!

READY FOR MORE GAMES?

More _Sammy the Golden Dog_ Books

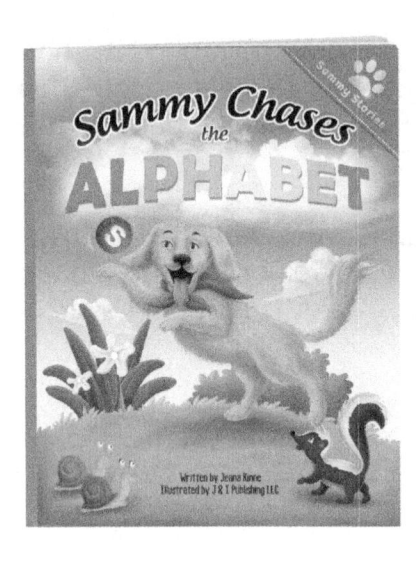

"Sammy Chases the Alphabet"
Teaching letters through play.

"Sammy Goes to Preschool"
Celebrating uniqueness among friends.

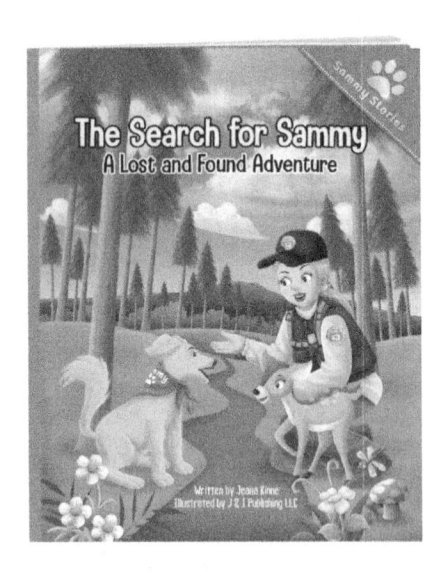

"The Search for Sammy"
Teaching safety skills if kids ever get lost.

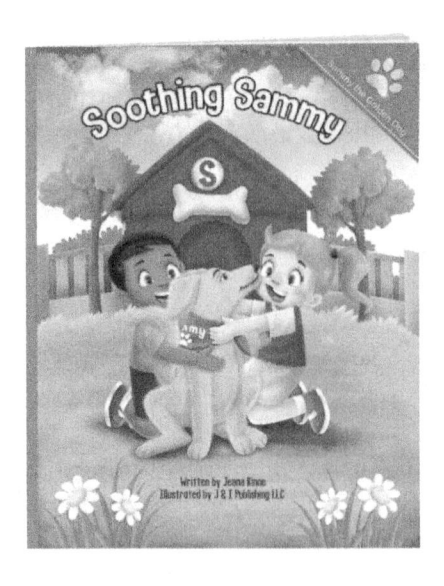

"Soothing Sammy"
Teaching calm down skills through play.

Available at www.JDEducational.com and Amazon.com

About the Author

Jeana Kinne (maiden name Downey) has worked in a variety of positions in the Early Childhood Education field. While attending Sonoma State University (SSU), Kinne worked at the campus preschool where she became passionate about creating quality preschool environments and developing enriched play-based curriculum.

Kinne received a Bachelor's degree in Sociology and Human Development, followed by a Master's degree in Education: Curriculum, Teaching and Learning with an emphasis in Child Psychology. She has since held a variety of positions within the Child Development field – including Preschool Teacher, Preschool Director, Early Childhood Behavioral Specialist, Preschool Consultation Specialist, Parenting Education and Early Intervention Specialist (working with infants and toddlers with developmental delays). She is also a guest lecturer at the local Community college.

Through working with parents and other Early Childhood Education professionals, it became clear that a parent's engagement in their child's academic and social development is a key component to the child's continued success. Kinne created this Curriculum Series to provide parents with an opportunity to become actively engaged in their child's development, enhancing their school readiness skills.

Made in United States
Orlando, FL
03 April 2023